MARTHA ROSE SHULMAN

Classic
Finger Foods
& Appetizers

Martha Rose Shulman

Classic Finger Foods & Appetizers

DK

DORLING KINDERSLEY

London • New York • Stuttgart

A DORLING KINDERSLEY BOOK

Created and produced by
CARROLL & BROWN LIMITED
5 Lonsdale Road
London NW6 6RA

Project Editor Shirin Patel
Assistant Editors Anne Hildyard and Stella Vayne

Editorial Consultant Jeni Wright

Art Direction Chrissie Lloyd and Louisa Cameron
Designer Michael Dyer

Photography David Murray and Jules Selmes

Production Wendy Rogers and Amanda Mackie

Food Preparation by Eric Treuillé

First published in Great Britain in 1995
by Dorling Kindersley Limited,
9 Henrietta Street, London WC2E 8PS

A CIP catalogue record for this book is available from the
British Library.

ISBN 0-7513-0162-0

Reproduced by Colourscan, Singapore
Printed and bound in Italy by A. Mondadori, Verona

FOREWORD

★

I decided to make a career out of what I loved to do best – cooking and entertaining – one Sunday morning after I had given a huge party that had lasted through the night. I had spent most of my time that night replenishing the finger foods and appetizers, making sure they looked beautiful so that it felt as if the party would last forever. It was a great party, and afterwards I was absolutely sure that cooking was what I wanted to do.

My Sunday morning decision was not just the whim in a morning-after haze. Within the year, I had launched a catering service and was catering for weddings and parties, conferences, and other events. I learned how to cook for large groups. And more than anything, I learned about finger foods and appetizers, because that was the way we usually served our food. We would rent long tables, cover them with colourful cloths, and set out beautiful platters of food, following a timetable which I always drew up once I had decided on a menu.

My purpose here is to help make entertaining as fun for you as it is for me. The range of delicious possibilities when making finger foods is limitless, and this collection of recipes is just a beginning.

Martha Rose Shulman

CONTENTS

★

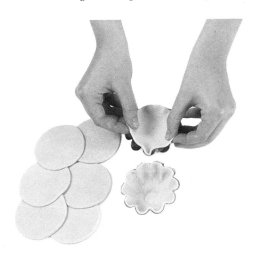

INTRODUCTION

★

Whether we entertain on a small or a large scale, formally or informally, today's choice is more often than not a buffet. We choose this style of entertaining because it's a lively, convivial one, that requires less fuss than more formal sit-down meals. Serving finger foods and tiny appetizers also gives us a wide range of menu choices: there can be enough dishes to make a substantial meal, or delicate morsels to precede one, or both.

The foods we are likely to serve are a far cry from the predictable canapés of yesteryear. Today our menus are light, colourful, and eclectic, with strong, ethnic flavours. So, side by side with traditional choux pastries, savoury quiches, and terrines, our party table is most likely to include Italian bruschetta (toasted country bread with garlic and olive oil) with an assortment of robust vegetable toppings, crisp Middle-Eastern filo triangles filled with spinach and feta cheese, buckwheat blini topped with smoked salmon or gravadlax, and gingery spring rolls filled with prawns and coriander. We might find platters of spicy Mexican nachos or Japanese-inspired sushi rolls, as well as Indonesian-style kebabs.

These days we seem to have less time than ever, so if we want to cook and entertain, we have to find ways to save time without sacrificing quality. That's why you'll find many recipes here for dishes such as frittatas and pizzas that can be made in one large pan, then cut into bite-sized portions. There are also plenty of suggestions for ready-made items that can be used as fillings and toppings. For example, a good bottled pesto can be spread on crostini and topped with a cooked prawn or scallop, then garnished with a fresh herb sprig, for a beautiful hors d'oeuvre that can be assembled in minutes. You'll find time-savers like this throughout the book. Today's buffets also reflect our growing concern with health and our new-found appreciation for fresh produce. Appetizers used to be filled with high-fat calories – nuts and cheese, chips served with soured-cream-based dips, vol-au-vents, and fried foods. Today, guests want lighter choices. Although this collection includes some

Aïoli Platter

high-protein dishes (the terrines, pâtés, and fish, for example), the greater number of recipes are based on vegetables and low-fat fish, poultry, and meat, such as ceviche and saté. This doesn't mean that they are not substantial. Colourful omelettes filled with red peppers and fresh peas or spinach and fresh herbs, nachos topped with shredded chicken and green tomatillo salsa or black beans, pungent, gingery tuna and aubergine kebabs are all extremely satisfying, but they won't make your guests feel that they have over-indulged.

Desserts can also have a prominent place on a buffet table, and sometimes an entire party can be focused on them. The dessert recipes in this volume are a good balance of rich and light ingredients and flavours. Fruit is ever present, in tartlets, and on platters with creamy dips – the dessert equivalent of crudités.

*Lamb Terrine
en Gelée*

Planning a Buffet

Planning a buffet is like planning for an opening night. Your buffet will be your set, there will be a curtain time when the guests arrive, and when it's all over you will dismantle the set, that is, clear up, load the dishwasher or start the washing-up. Stage fright is often part of the bargain. Indeed, friends often tell me that they never enjoy their own parties.

But you can have a good time at your own party if you plan carefully. When planning the menu, consider the time available to you, and the amount of help you will have. If these are limited, don't plan to serve many time-consuming items, such as the wraps and rolls. Instead, make whole

frittatas and savoury quiches and cut them into bite-sized servings. Choose items that can be made in advance and frozen, such as blini or filo pastries. Serve platters of crudités with dips, bearing in mind that most crudités can be cut up in advance and kept in the refrigerator overnight. Have a mix of hot and cold dishes.

For dessert, you could buy petits fours, to serve with bowls of fruit. Sometimes I simply put a huge basket of tangerines on a party table, with an assortment of chocolates, small biscuits, and unsalted nuts.

*Spinach &
Feta Cheese
filo pastry parcel*

Choosing a Theme

Party food can have a theme – Italian, Mexican, or Middle Eastern, for example – or you can have an assortment of dishes from different countries. It's advisable not to serve too many different types of ethnic food at the same time, however. For instance, if you are serving several Oriental dishes, it's best not to serve nachos as well. Delicately seasoned dishes, such as quiches, frittatas, or carpaccios, won't clash with finger foods that have more pronounced flavours.

Appetizers as a prelude to a meal need not be very elaborate: a few tasty items will do, and these should not be too filling. If the dishes are for a cocktail or evening party they should be more substantial, because they

*Chicken
nachos*

may well be a substitute for dinner. For such an occasion, have five or more dishes, with a balance of protein-rich, vegetable, and high-carbohydrate items. Serve one or two kinds of savoury quiches or omelettes, a pâté or a selection of meatballs, or perhaps ceviche, stuffed vegetables or a platter of crudités with dips, bruschetta, and a platter of filo pastries. Party food should be easy to handle. Serve items easily eaten with one hand in a couple of bites, but provide places for guests to set down their drinks in case they need to use their other hand to deal with food.

Hot or Cold?

Whether you include hot food at your party depends in part on how substantial the selection is meant to be. I dislike chafing dishes (except for the very simple Bagna Cauda, which must be kept hot), because the food can become soggy. When I serve hot food, it is usually the type that is baked, then served straight from the oven, such as filo pastries or mushrooms filled with pesto.

It is easier to deal with hot food if you have help in the kitchen: you can host the party while your helpers watch the oven. However, as most of the dishes in this collection can be served at room temperature, you can choose only these for your party, if you cannot have help.

Arranging the Table

Food should look colourful and enticing on a party table. Use attractive platters, plates, baskets, and bowls for displaying food, and garnish foods that are not naturally bright in colour with sprigs of fresh herbs, radish roses, cherry tomatoes, chillies, or lemon or lime wedges.

I like to pass round some of the dishes on smaller plates and platters, so that guests don't have to crowd around the party table. If space is limited, you can fit a large number of items on a table if you alternate platters and plates in a zigzag pattern. Put out knives to spread foods such as hummus and pâtés, and arrange napkins within easy reach of dishes such as stuffed vegetables and dips.

Platters should look as if they have just been set out, so they should be replenished as soon as they are half empty – bring out replacements on smaller plates. Regularly remove empty bottles, paper plates, and full ashtrays.

Organization

The key to successful entertaining is planning. Once you have decided on your menu, make lists. I make two lists when I entertain: a shopping list, and a calendar, with the menu written at the top, and all the tasks assigned to a particular day. If the party is a very large one, I may also make a list of equipment and serving dishes and utensils I know I will need. I try to begin as far ahead of time as possible. If there is something that can be

*Mini Fruit
Sandwiches*

frozen, for instance pizza crust or pastry for quiches and tartlets, blini, and filo pastries, I make it at least a week in advance. Dishes that can be frozen are often time-consuming items, so it's good to prepare them beforehand.

I try to do all the shopping by the day of the party; the exception is, of course, fish or raw or marinated meats, but these items can be ordered, so all I have to do is to pick them up. I also set up my party table and bar, and arrange flowers, the night before. There is something comforting about the room looking ready well in advance.

A Party Check List

Decide the date and time

Plan guest list

Send out invitations

Plan menu

Check recipes to make in advance
  and freeze

Assess space, tables, chairs

Assess number of dishes, glasses,
  plates, cutlery, and serving dishes

Make shopping list for
  food and drinks (including
  coffee and tea)

Make ice

Prepare dishes

Chill wine

Arrange flowers

Arrange table

Tips for Storing Food

Storing food in limited refrigerator space can be tricky, but the more that can be stored, the more can be prepared in advance. Plastic bags are space savers. Except for raw carrots, celery, and radishes, which must be kept in cold water, prepared raw vegetables and blanched and steamed vegetables can be sealed in plastic bags. To keep herbs fresh, cut the stalks off about 5 mm (1/4 in) from the ends, wrap the ends of the stalks in dampened paper towels, then wrap them tightly in foil. Seal in a plastic bag. Cheese can be grated and bagged. Store dips and spreads in jars in the refrigerator door, or in containers that can be stacked. To store made-up platters of food, stand corks on the platters, higher than the surface of the food, and cover: the corks will hold the covering off the food like a tent.

Quantities and Quantity Cooking

I always count on guests having at least 2–3 items of each dish at a buffet. Most of the recipes in this book serve 10 people, and some serve up to 20. All the recipes can be multiplied to serve larger groups, but remember to allow more time for preparation, even for simple dishes. If you are serving individual wraps and rolls or are having more than 10 guests, I recommend that you enlist someone to help you. Knowing that there will be somebody to assist with preparation, serving, and keeping it all looking good will help you relax and enjoy your own party even more.

DRINKS

★

A glass of chilled white or fizzy wine or a cocktail will get any party off to a good start and help guests to relax. When entertaining, it is a good idea to have plenty of alcoholic and non-alcoholic drinks. However, you will find serving and refilling easier if there is a limited choice. If you can, buy more drink than is needed on a sale or return basis.

Cool and Collected

A practical point worth considering is to make sure there are plenty of corkscrews and bottle openers so that more than one person can open drinks. Plenty of ice is essential: make it in advance or buy it ready-made from off-licences. When the weather is cold, wines can be stored outside to chill, otherwise, if space in the refrigerator is limited, bottles can be kept cool in the bath or in buckets filled with ice and water.

Separate Tables

Arrange a separate table for drinks so that the food tables don't get too crowded. It helps if someone is in charge of serving drinks, at least initially. Or have glasses of wine or Champagne ready to offer around on a tray.

Happy Hour

When guests arrive, welcome them with an aperitif, such as kir made with crème de cassis and dry white wine; Pimms; Champagne; or Buck's Fizz. Once food is served, offer a choice of chilled white wine, red wine, or a home-made punch. Your choice of wine will be determined by factors such as your budget, your personal preferences, or the type of food that is being served.

Wine Choice

In general, for drinks parties, sparkling wines, or white wines, such as Chardonnay and Sancerre, or light reds, such as Fleurie or Valpolicella, are very acceptable. For brunches, Champagne or Buck's Fizz are ideal. At lunch time, pick light wines, such as Vinho Verde, Bordeaux, or a dry rosé. With a meaty meal, choose full-bodied reds, such as Chianti, Barolo, or an Australian Cabernet Sauvignon.

Speciality Drinks

For the themed parties suggested in this book, it is fun to serve an appropriate drink:

Middle-Eastern Mezze: Buzbag (a full-bodied Turkish red wine), Arak (an aniseed-flavoured aperitif) or Turkish coffee.
A French Buffet: Kir or Kir Royale, Noilly Prat, or Dubonnet.
Celebrating Italy: Martini, Campari, Punt e Mes, Frascati, or Soave.
A Feast from the Orient: Rice wine, beer, Jasmine or Pekoe Blossom tea.
A Mexican Fiesta: Tequila or Margaritas.
A Summer Party: Pimms, Summer Fruit Punch, or Piña Colada Punch (see page 13).

Cocktails often taste deceptively light, but can actually be quite lethal in their effect, so it is best to be judicious about mixing spirits.

A good stock of soft drinks is advisable, such as soda water, tomato juice, fizzy and still mineral water, cola, and fruit juices.

AVERAGE DRINK QUANTITIES

Drink	1 person	10 people	20 people	50 people
Wine	½ bottle	5 bottles	10 bottles	25 bottles
Punch or Mulled Wine	150 ml/¼ pint	1.5 litres/2½ pints	3 litres/5 pints	6 litres/10 pints
Sparkling wine or Champagne	⅓ bottle	4 bottles	8 bottles	16 bottles
Buck's Fizz: Champagne	75 ml/2½ fl oz	1¼ bottles	2½ bottles	6 bottles
Orange juice	45ml/1½ fl oz	450 ml/¾ pint	900 ml/1½ pints	2·5 litres/4 pints
Spirits	75 ml/2½ fl oz	1 bottle	2 bottles	5 bottles

SUMMER PARTY PUNCH

Makes 2.75 litres (4½ pints)

INGREDIENTS

500 g (1 lb) dessert apples, cored and sliced
300 ml (½ pint) orange liqueur
150 ml (¼ pint) brandy
1 orange, thinly sliced
1 lemon, thinly sliced
250 g (8 oz) strawberries, sliced
3 bottles of sparkling wine
ice cubes
mint and lemon verbena sprigs for decoration

PREPARATION

1 Put the apple slices in a large punch bowl. Stir in the liqueur and brandy. Cover and chill in the refrigerator for at least 2 hours.
2 Add the orange and lemon slices to the bowl about 1 hour before serving.
3 Just before serving, add the strawberries, sparkling wine, and ice cubes. Mix well and decorate with mint and lemon verbena sprigs.

MULLED WINE

Makes about 6.5 litres (11 pints)

INGREDIENTS

1.8 litres (3 pints) water
625 g (1¼) lb caster sugar
6 cloves
2 cinnamon sticks
2 lemons, thinly sliced
peeled zest of 1 lemon
6 bottles red wine, Burgundy or claret
lemon slices to decorate

PREPARATION

1 Bring the water, sugar, and spices to a boil in a large pan. Add the lemon slices and lemon zest, stir well, and leave to stand for 10 minutes or until the sugar has dissolved.
2 Add the red wine and warm through: do not boil.
3 Strain into a warmed punch bowl and serve hot, decorated with lemon slices.

PINA COLADA PUNCH

The popular West-Indian cocktail of pineapple and cream of coconut is here converted to a lighter punch.
Makes about 6.5 litres (11 pints)

INGREDIENTS

3 tbsp brown sugar
5-cm (2-in) piece dried root ginger, crushed
600 ml (1 pint) water
250 g (8 oz) desiccated coconut
1.25 litres (2 pints) boiling water
600 ml (1 pint) dark rum
2.5 litres (4 pints) pineapple juice
cocktail cherries, pineapple chunks, and ice to decorate

PREPARATION

1 Put the sugar, ginger, and the cold water in a pan, bring to a boil, and simmer for 1–2 minutes. Let cool and strain into a serving bowl.
2 Meanwhile, mix together the coconut and boiling water in another pan and let stand for 10 minutes.
3 Strain the coconut mixture into the serving bowl and mix well. Stir in the rum and pineapple juice and chill for at least 2 hours. Serve decorated with cocktail cherries, pineapple chunks and ice.

Menu Planning

Whatever the occasion, large or small, informal or smart, indoors or out, a buffet-style party with a range of finger foods and appetizers is ideal. Here are some menu suggestions for different types of entertaining.

★

Just One Course

Appetizers and finger foods are very adaptable. They can make up the whole of a meal or just a part of it. For a simple menu, serve a selection of only savoury or sweet dishes.

Just Starters

★

Smoked Trout Devilled Eggs (page 42)

Herbed Goat's Cheese Crêpes (page 54)

Roast Pepper & Mozzarella Crostini (page 70)

Prawn & Tomato Nachos (page 82)

Mussels on the Half Shell (page 102)

Lamb Terrine en Gelée (page 112)

★

Just Desserts

★

Fresh Fruit Tartlets (page 114)

Rich Pecan Squares (page 118)

Coffee Cream Puffs (page 120)

Celebration Brownies (page 124)

Biscotti with Raisins (page 126)

Mini Fruit Sandwiches (page 130)

Summer Fruit Platter (page 132)

★

Lamb Terrine en Gelée

Fresh Fruit Tartlets

COCKTAIL PARTIES

One of the easiest ways to entertain a large number of guests
is at a cocktail party. The menus are interchangeable for a
luncheon or evening party. The weather may dictate whether
hot or cold appetizers should be served, but whichever
are chosen, it is always best to serve plenty of titbits with
drinks, and to include some which are high in protein.

COLD SPREAD

★

Ceviche

Baba Ghanoush (page 30)

Aïoli Platter (page 32)

Tender Pea & Pepper Frittata (page 39)

Olive Focaccia (page 67)

Rice & Meat Dolmades (page 78)

Chicken Nachos with Salsa Verde (page 83)

Ceviche (page 104)

Almond Biscotti (page 126)

★

HOT SPREAD

★

Blini with Corn & Tomato Salsa (page 47)

Spinach Quiche (page 58)

Wild Mushroom & Herb Pizza (page 65)

Anchovy Bruschetta (page 71)

*Leek & Feta Cheese Filo Pastries
(page 77)*

Spinach & Tofu Wontons (page 88)

Prawn & Pepper Kebabs (page 98)

Rhubarb & Honey Tartlets (page 116)

★

Rhubarb & Honey Tartlets

BRUNCH & LUNCH

An informal brunch or lunch is an ideal opportunity for
relaxed entertaining. Mid-morning brunch combines the best
of breakfast and lunch, and a selection of new-wave dishes,
such as frittata and sushi, will add a stylish touch. For lunch,
choose more substantial dishes, such as the hot dip, Bagna
Cauda, or Chicken & Pepper Kebabs.

ELEGANT BRUNCH

★

Smoked Salmon & Dill Frittata (page 38)

Tapenade Devilled Eggs (page 43)

*Blini with Caviar & Fromage Blanc
(page 46)*

Platter of Quiches (page 58)

*Wild Mushroom Bruschetta
(page 72)*

Cucumber Sushi (page 84)

Cherry Clafoutis Tartlets (page 119)

★

LIGHT LUNCH

★

Bagna Cauda (page 30)

Herb & Spring Onion Quiche (page 58)

Sage & Onion Focaccia (page 67)

*Lamb & Green Vegetable
Filo Pastries (page 77)*

Black Bean Nachos (page 82)

Crunchy Tofu Soft Spring Rolls (page 92)

Chicken & Pepper Kebabs (page 98)

Fresh Fruit & Cream Puffs (page 120)

★

Platter of Quiches

Fresh Fruit & Cream Puffs

DINNER PARTIES

Whether entertaining family, friends, or business associates,
a dinner party should be fairly substantial, and when it
consists of finger foods, there should be 2–3 of each item per
guest. If the celebration is on a grander scale, many dishes
can be prepared in advance to make the whole affair
as stylish as possible.

SPECIAL OCCASION DINNER

★

*Blini with Smoked Salmon & Fromage Blanc
(page 46)*

Fresh Herb Crostini (page 70)

Chicken Nachos with Salsa Verde (page 83)

Chicken & Pepper Kebabs (page 98)

Clams on the Half Shell (page 102)

Lemon Sablés (page 127)

Chocolate Meringues (page 130)

★

Clams on the Half Shell

BUFFET FOR 50

★

3 quantities Aïoli Platter (page 34)

4 quantities Asparagus Frittata (page 39)

*2 quantities Smoked Trout Devilled Eggs
(page 42)*

50 Blini with Green Tomatillo Salsa (page 47)

*2 quantities Chicken Provençal Gougères
(page 51)*

*3 quantities Courgette & Red Pepper Quiche
(page 58)*

*3 quantities Tomato
& Olive Bruschetta (page 70)*

*4 quantities Tuna & Red Pepper Kebabs
with Ginger-Soy Marinade (page 99)*

3 quantities Gravadlax (page 104)

*2 quantities Cranberry-Pear
Tartlets (page 119)*

*2 quantities Fresh Fruit
& Cream Puffs (page 120)*

1 quantity Ginger Biscotti (page 126)

2 quantities Chocolate Fancies (page 130)

★

EATING ALFRESCO

Food always tastes better eaten outdoors. Dishes can be
prepared in advance and transported with the minimum of fuss,
if properly packaged. Take advantage of the location
and have a barbecue. If the party is to be held nearer home, in a
garden or around a pool, you can include hot food
ready from the kitchen.

PICNIC

★

Herb Pot Pourri Devilled Eggs (page 42)

Goat's Cheese & Pepper Gougères (page 50)

Olive Focaccia (page 67)

Rice & Herb Dolmades (page 78)

California Sushi (page 84)

Smoked Duck Soft Spring Rolls (page 93)

Chocolate Chip Cookies (page 127)

Lemon Sablés (page 127)

★

Soft & Crispy Spring Rolls

GARDEN OR POOL PARTY

★

Courgette & Red Pepper Frittata (page 38)

*Blue Cheese & Pear Gougères
(page 50)*

Oriental-style Crab Crêpes (page 52)

*Tomato & Caper Bruschetta
(page 71)*

Beef & Chicken Saté (page 98)

Middle-Eastern Meatballs (page 99)

Raspberry Clafoutis Tartlets (page 119)

Mexican Fruit Platter (page 132)

★

Mexican Fruit Platter

VEGETABLES

*I don't think I've ever given a party without including
vegetables in some form. They may make up an
attractive platter of crudités with one or more dips,
or I serve just a few, such as cucumbers and red
peppers, with a hummus or smoked trout filling.
Vegetarian dishes can be truly exciting, given the wide
variety of vegetables, exotic and familiar, that is now
available, and the range of flavours I have included.
Stuff mushrooms with pesto, cherry tomatoes
with herbed goat's cheese, or serve baby new
potatoes with caviar.*

STUFFED VEGETABLES

No matter how you serve vegetables, they always provide a party table with a colourful focus. Raw vegetables filled with a variety of stuffings provide contrasting and refreshing textures. You can spoon the stuffing into the vegetable containers as shown in the picture here, but you can also pipe it in.

A FEAST OF VEGETABLES

On the platter are Courgette Boats filled with Tunisian Courgette Purée and garnished with a sprinkling of paprika, Tomato Cups filled with Green Olive & Almond Tapenade and garnished with sliced olives and chopped herbs, and Cucumber Rings filled with Tzatziki and garnished with dill.

TO MAKE STUFFED VEGETABLES

500 ml (16 fl oz) stuffing fills approximately 1 kg (2 lb) vegetables

1 Choose vegetables for stuffing from those suggested on page 25. See also page 148.

2 Make the raw vegetables into containers by simply hollowing them out for cups or boats, or by blanching or cooking them before shaping, as directed on page 148.

3 Prepare your choice of stuffing from the recipes given on pages 22–25. Chill the stuffing until you are ready to fill the vegetable containers.

4 Spoon or pipe the stuffing into the containers. If serving the stuffed vegetables warm, heat through in a preheated 200°C (400°F, Gas 6) oven for 10–15 minutes.

Baby aubergine halves filled with Tunisian Courgette Purée and sprinkled with paprika

STUFFINGS FOR VEGETABLES

The textures and colours of stuffings should complement their vegetable containers.
For maximum variety, mix and match the recipes below with suitable vegetables
(see pages 25 and 148).

★

GREEN OLIVE & ALMOND TAPENADE

This is a lighter — and somewhat unorthodox — version of
the olive paste named after the Provençal for caper —
tapéno. Traditionally, it contains anchovy and tuna, but
I have omitted the fish and added almonds.
Makes 500 ml (16 fl oz)

INGREDIENTS

2 large garlic cloves, peeled
250 g (8 oz) green Provençal or Greek olives, stoned
30 g (1 oz) blanched almonds
1 1/2 tbsp capers, drained and rinsed
1 tsp fresh thyme leaves, or 1/2 tsp dried thyme
1 tsp fresh chopped rosemary,
or 1/2 tsp crumbled dried rosemary
3 tbsp olive oil
2 tbsp lemon juice
freshly ground black pepper

PREPARATION

1 Turn on a food processor fitted with the metal
blade, and drop in the garlic. When it is chopped,
turn off the machine and add the olives, almonds,
capers, thyme, and rosemary. Turn on the
machine, and work together until fairly smooth.
2 Add the olive oil and lemon juice, and continue
working until the mixture forms a uniform
paste. Add pepper, to taste.

—— *Making Tapenade by Hand* ——

Tapenade can be made in a pestle and mortar instead of in a
food processor. Pound together the garlic, olives, almonds, and
capers. Add the herbs, pound to a paste, and slowly add the
olive oil, 1 tbsp at a time, working it into the mixture after
each addition. Slowly work in the lemon juice, 1 tbsp at a
time, to form a uniform paste. Add pepper, to taste.

TZATZIKI

This pungent mixture of cucumber, yogurt, and garlic
is especially good as a stuffing for cucumbers, beetroots,
and red peppers, but in Greece, where the
recipe originated, it is more often used as a dip
for pitta bread.
Makes 900 ml–1 litre (1 1/2 –1 3/4 pints)

INGREDIENTS

1 cucumber, peeled and very finely chopped or grated
salt and freshly ground pepper
500 ml (16 fl oz) drained yogurt (see page 156)
3 garlic cloves, crushed
2 tbsp lemon juice

PREPARATION

1 Toss the cucumber with a generous amount
of salt, and let stand in a colander for 1 hour.
Rinse under cold water and squeeze dry.
2 Beat the yogurt in a bowl with a whisk until
smooth. Stir in the cucumber, garlic, lemon
juice, and salt and pepper to taste.

CAVIAR

The better the quality of caviar you use (see box, page 46),
the more luxurious this stuffing will be.
Makes 250 ml (8 fl oz)

INGREDIENTS

125 ml (4 fl oz) fromage blanc, plain low-fat yogurt,
or soured cream
125 g (4 oz) black caviar

PREPARATION

1 Fill each vegetable container with fromage blanc,
yogurt, or soured cream.
2 Top with 1/2 heaped tsp of caviar.

TUNISIAN COURGETTE PUREE

This stuffing uses harissa, *a very hot, North African paste made from chillies, garlic, cumin, coriander, and caraway seeds. It is available in small cans and tubes from delicatessens and Middle-Eastern speciality stores. Always use harissa with caution – it is fiery.*
Makes 750 ml (1¼ pints)

INGREDIENTS

500 g (1 lb) courgettes, sliced
2 large garlic cloves, crushed in a pestle and mortar or garlic press
2 tbsp olive oil
¾ tsp ground caraway seeds
¼ tsp harissa *or ⅛ tsp cayenne pepper*
2–4 tbsp lemon juice
salt and freshly ground pepper

PREPARATION

1 Steam the courgettes for 10–15 minutes, until they are thoroughly tender. Drain and rinse under cold running water.
2 Squeeze out as much moisture as possible from the courgettes and transfer them to a food processor fitted with the metal blade. Work until smooth.
3 Add the remaining ingredients to the food processor, with lemon juice and salt and pepper to taste. Work together until evenly mixed, then taste, and adjust seasonings.

If you make this courgette stuffing several hours in advance, reserve the lemon juice and add it shortly before serving. If it is added in advance, it will spoil the bright green colour of the courgettes.

Harissa

BRANDADE

Brandade is a salt cod purée from France. It makes a lovely stuffing for tomatoes and peppers.
Makes 500 ml (16 fl oz)

INGREDIENTS

500 g (1 lb) salt cod, dried or fresh
2 litres (3½ pints) water
2 medium onions, quartered
5 large garlic cloves, 3 cut in half, 2 finely chopped
2 bay leaves
175 ml (6 fl oz) milk
4 tbsp olive oil
freshly ground pepper

PREPARATION

1 Place the fish in a large bowl and cover with water. If convenient, put the bowl in the kitchen sink and keep the water running in a thin stream so that the water in the bowl is constantly renewed. Alternatively, change the soaking water several times over 48 hours for dried salt cod, or over 24 hours for fresh salt cod.
2 Cut the cod into a few large pieces and place in a large, heavy-based saucepan. Add the water, onions, halved garlic cloves, and the bay leaves. Bring slowly to a simmer over medium-low heat.
3 As soon as the water reaches a simmer and before it comes to a boil, cover the pan, and turn off the heat. Let stand for 10 minutes. Drain the fish and transfer to a bowl. Let stand until cool enough to handle.
4 Remove the bones and skin from the fish. Flake the flesh by rubbing it between your fingers or using a fork or wooden spoon, checking for any hidden small bones. Transfer to a food processor fitted with the metal blade.
5 Scald the milk in a small saucepan, remove from the heat, and add half of the olive oil.
6 Heat the remaining oil in a heavy-based saucepan over medium-low heat and add the finely chopped garlic. As soon as the garlic begins to sizzle, remove the pan from the heat, and transfer the garlic and oil to the food processor.
7 Turn on the food processor and add the milk and oil mixture in a slow stream, until the cod has absorbed all of the liquid it can. Continue to process until the cod mixture is fluffy, adding pepper to taste.

Tomato Cups (page 148) stuffed with Herbed Goat's Cheese

HERBED GOAT'S CHEESE

This recipe can also be used as a dip or topping.
It will keep for a few hours in the refrigerator.
Makes about 500 ml (16 fl oz)

INGREDIENTS

250 g (8 oz) low-fat cottage cheese
250 g (8 oz) goat's cheese
4–6 tbsp plain low-fat yogurt
2 garlic cloves, finely chopped or crushed
30 g (1 oz) fresh herbs, such as parsley, tarragon, basil,
dill, chives, chervil, or oregano, finely chopped
salt and freshly ground pepper

PREPARATION

Combine the cheeses, 4 tbsp yogurt, and the garlic in a food processor fitted with the metal blade. Process until smooth, adding more yogurt if desired. Transfer to a bowl and stir in the herbs, salt if necessary, and pepper to taste.

GOAT'S CHEESE WITH SUN-DRIED TOMATO

Use this stuffing to top blini (see pages 44–47)
and fill crêpes (see pages 52–53) also if you prefer.
It will keep for up to 3 days in the refrigerator.
Makes about 500 ml (16 fl oz)

INGREDIENTS

250 g (8 oz) low-fat cottage cheese
250 g (8 oz) goat's cheese
4–6 tbsp plain low-fat yogurt
2 garlic cloves, finely chopped or crushed
90 g (3 oz) oil-packed sun-dried tomatoes,
drained and chopped
salt and freshly ground pepper

PREPARATION

Combine the cheeses, 4 tbsp yogurt, and the garlic in a food processor fitted with the metal blade. Process until smooth, adding more yogurt if desired. Transfer to a bowl and stir in the sun-dried tomatoes, and salt and pepper to taste.

NORTH-AFRICAN-STYLE TUNA

Mint and cumin lend an exotic flavour to this stuffing. It
will keep for 1 day in the refrigerator.
Makes about 500 ml (16 fl oz)

INGREDIENTS

2 x 173-g (6^{1}/8-oz) cans water-packed tuna, drained
2 shallots or 1 bunch of spring onions, both white and
green parts, finely chopped
60–125 ml (2–4 fl oz) plain low-fat yogurt
4 tbsp lemon juice
2 garlic cloves, finely chopped or crushed
4 tbsp chopped fresh mint
^{1}/2 tsp ground cumin
salt and freshly ground pepper

PREPARATION

Break up the tuna into flakes and mash with a fork. Mix in the remaining ingredients, using the smaller amount of yogurt first. The mixture should be fairly smooth; add more yogurt as desired. Taste, and adjust seasonings.

SMOKED TROUT PUREE

It couldn't be simpler to purée the smoked trout with
the other ingredients in a food processor. All you need is
excellent smoked trout – pink salmon trout makes the
prettiest purée. It will keep for up to 3 days
in the refrigerator.
Makes about 325 ml (11 fl oz)

INGREDIENTS

250 g (8 oz) smoked trout
4 tbsp plain low-fat yogurt or fromage blanc (see page 156)
2–3 tbsp lemon juice
1 tbsp crème fraîche
1 tsp Dijon mustard
salt and freshly ground pepper

PREPARATION

Remove any skin and bones from the trout. Break the flesh into pieces, place in a food processor fitted with the metal blade, and chop. Add the remaining ingredients except the salt, adjust the lemon juice to taste, and purée until smooth. Taste, and add salt if necessary.

BASIL PESTO

*Pesto isn't just for pasta. Use it to stuff vegetable containers
such as cherry tomatoes and mushrooms.
Makes about 175 ml (6 fl oz)*

INGREDIENTS

*2 large garlic cloves, peeled
2 tbsp pine nuts
60 g (2 oz) fresh basil
1/4–1/2 tsp salt
90 ml (3 fl oz) olive oil
60 g (2 oz) Parmesan cheese, freshly grated
2 tbsp grated pecorino cheese
freshly ground pepper*

PREPARATION

1 Turn on a food processor fitted with the metal
blade and drop in the garlic. When it is chopped,
turn off the machine, and add the pine nuts,
basil, and salt to taste. Turn on the machine and
work together; with the machine running, add
the olive oil. Work until the mixture is smooth,
stopping the machine from time to time to wipe
any basil leaves down from the side of the bowl.

2 Add the cheeses and pepper to taste and mix
together well.

VARIATION

CORIANDER PESTO: Substitute *60 g (2 oz) fresh
coriander* for the basil, or *a combination of 30 g (1 oz)
fresh coriander, 15 g (1/2 oz) fresh basil, and 15 g
(1/2 oz) fresh flat-leaf parsley.*

 *Pesto freezes well. Work the herbs with the pine nuts,
salt, and olive oil. Do not add the garlic, cheeses, or
pepper until you defrost the pesto.*

Making Pesto by Hand

*Both Basil and Coriander Pesto can be made in a pestle
and mortar instead of in a food processor. Pound together the
garlic and pine nuts. Add the herbs and salt, pound to a
paste, and slowly add the olive oil, 1 tbsp at a time, working
it into the mixture after each addition. Work in the cheeses
and adjust seasonings to taste.*

Vegetable Containers

*Many vegetables, in addition to those shaped into
containers on pages 148, lend themselves to becoming
colourful and complementary receptacles for stuffings.*

BABY MARROW BOWLS: *Cut baby marrows in half
crossways and blanch in a pan of boiling salted water.
Carefully scoop out some flesh from each half, leaving a
1-cm (1/2-in) border all around.*

RED PEPPER CUPS: *Cut each pepper in half crossways.
Core and scoop out the seeds.*

MANGETOUT PURSES: *Blanch mangetout in a large pan
of boiling salted water. Carefully slit open the curved side
of each pod.*

BABY BEETROOT CUPS: *Cook scrubbed beetroot in boiling
salted water for 20–30 minutes. Drain, and let cool. Peel and
trim, and cut a very thin slice off each beetroot base so that the
beetroot stand upright. Hollow out each beetroot with a melon
baller, or cut out a conical shape with a sharp knife.*

MUSHROOM CUPS: *To prepare the mushrooms for baking
with a filling in them, simply twist off the stalks, and rinse
or wipe the caps. If the mushrooms are to have a cold filling,
place them, rounded-side down, on ungreased baking trays
in a preheated 220°C (425°F, Gas 7) oven, and bake for
10 minutes.*

SMALL POTATO CUPS: *Scrub, but do not peel, small
potatoes. Cook them in boiling salted water for about
20 minutes, until tender. Drain, and let cool. Cut them in
half, and cut a very thin slice off the rounded end of each of
the halves so that they stand upright. Hollow out each potato
half with a melon baller, or cut out a conical shape with a
sharp paring knife.*

LETTUCE LEAF SAUCERS: *Wash the small inner leaves of
lettuces, and dry them well.*

Baby marrow   *Baby red pepper*

Mangetout   *Baby marrow*

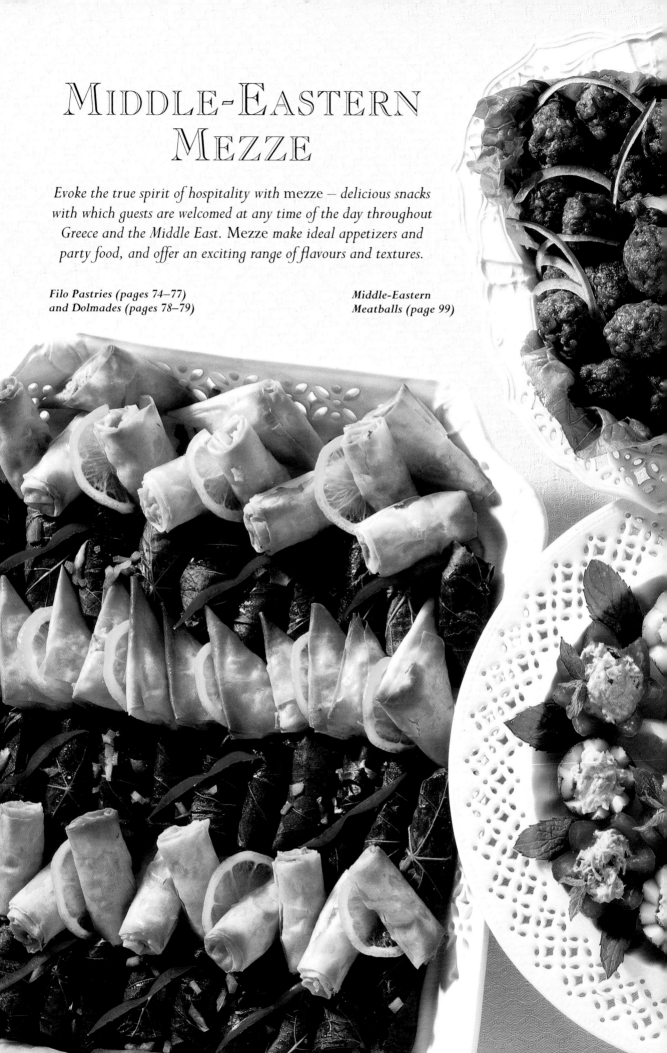

MIDDLE-EASTERN MEZZE

*Evoke the true spirit of hospitality with mezze – delicious snacks
with which guests are welcomed at any time of the day throughout
Greece and the Middle East. Mezze make ideal appetizers and
party food, and offer an exciting range of flavours and textures.*

*Filo Pastries (pages 74–77)
and Dolmades (pages 78–79)*

*Middle-Eastern
Meatballs (page 99)*

Tomato and Courgette
Cups (page 148) with
North-African-style
Tuna stuffing (page 24)

Apricot & Almond
Tartlets (page 118)

Hummus (page 30)
in pepper cups with
pitta bread

DIPS FOR VEGETABLES

A selection of dips served with raw vegetables or crudités arranged on a large platter makes an eye-catching item. Dips are ideal for serving at parties because they can be prepared up to a day in advance and kept tightly covered in the refrigerator. A number of the dips given here are spicy or piquant – perfect for pepping up subtle vegetable flavours. Choose your vegetable dippers from the suggestions given for the Aïoli Platter (see pages 32–33) and from the selection on page 149.

★

MAYONNAISE

I always make mayonnaise in a food processor because it's so quick and easy – and foolproof. This recipe is for a basic mayonnaise, the most classic of dips. You can add chopped fresh herbs just before serving if you prefer.
Makes 350 ml (12 fl oz)

INGREDIENTS

1 large egg
2 tsp red or white wine vinegar or sherry vinegar
1 tsp Dijon mustard
salt and freshly ground pepper
125 ml (4 fl oz) olive oil
250 ml (8 fl oz) sunflower or rapeseed oil
1–2 tbsp lemon juice

PREPARATION

1 Put the egg, wine or sherry vinegar, mustard, and 1/2 tsp salt in the bowl of a food processor fitted with the metal blade. Work until all the ingredients are evenly combined.
2 With the food processor running, slowly add the olive oil a drop at a time, then add the sunflower or rapeseed oil in a very thin stream, until all of it has been absorbed. Add lemon juice and pepper to taste.

ASIAN SESAME-GINGER DIP

Makes 250 ml (8 fl oz)

INGREDIENTS

175 ml (6 fl oz) drained yogurt (see page 156)
4 tbsp sesame oil
1 tbsp lemon or lime juice
1 tbsp rice wine vinegar
1 tbsp balsamic vinegar
1 small garlic clove, finely chopped or crushed
2 tsp finely chopped fresh root ginger
2–3 tsp soy sauce
salt and freshly ground pepper

PREPARATION

Combine all the ingredients, adding soy sauce, salt, and pepper to taste.

CREAMY CURRIED DIP

Makes 350 ml (12 fl oz)

INGREDIENTS

175 ml (6 fl oz) plain low-fat yogurt
175 ml (6 fl oz) mayonnaise
1 1/2 tsp curry powder
1/2 tsp turmeric
1/2 tsp chilli powder
1/4 tsp ground ginger
1/4 tsp paprika
salt and freshly ground pepper

PREPARATION

Combine all the ingredients, adding salt and pepper to taste.

FRESH TOMATO SALSA

Jalapeño peppers vary in intensity from mild to hot. If you are not sure of their strength, add them sparingly and adjust the flavour of the salsa by adding extra peppers after tasting.
Makes about 600 ml (1 pint)

INGREDIENTS

1 kg (2 lb) tomatoes, chopped
1/2 small red onion, finely chopped
1 tbsp red wine vinegar or balsamic vinegar
2–3 jalapeño or serrano peppers, cored, seeded, and finely chopped
4–5 tbsp chopped fresh coriander
salt and freshly ground pepper

PREPARATION

Combine all the ingredients, adding jalapeño peppers, coriander, salt, and pepper to taste.

TAHINI-YOGURT DIP

Makes 400 ml (14 fl oz)

INGREDIENTS

250 ml (8 fl oz) plain low-fat yogurt
6 tbsp sesame tahini
4 tbsp lemon juice
1–2 large garlic cloves, finely chopped or crushed
1/2–1 tsp ground cumin
salt and freshly ground pepper

PREPARATION

Whisk together all the ingredients, adding the garlic, cumin, salt, and pepper to taste. Adjust seasonings, and thin out, if required, with water.

Creamy Curried Dip

Fresh Tomato Salsa

Tahini-Yogurt Dip

HUMMUS

Hummus, the Middle-Eastern chick-pea purée, is delicious,
easy to make, and can be prepared well in advance –
in fact, it tastes better when made at least 1 day ahead.
Serves about 10

INGREDIENTS

2 large garlic cloves, peeled
250 g (8 oz) dried chick peas, soaked, cooked, and drained
(with some liquid reserved)
or 475-g (15-oz) can of chick peas, drained
(with some liquid reserved)
2–3 tbsp plain low-fat yogurt
4 tbsp lemon juice
3 tbsp sesame tahini
2–3 tbsp olive oil
1/2 tsp ground cumin
salt
red and green peppers for serving (optional)

PREPARATION

1 Turn on a food processor fitted with the metal
blade, and drop in the garlic. When it is
chopped, turn off the machine, and add the chick
peas. Process for about 30 seconds, until roughly
chopped and grainy.

2 Add 2 tbsp yogurt with the lemon juice,
tahini, 2 tbsp oil, cumin, and salt to taste, and
process until smooth.

3 Scrape down the side of the processor bowl
and check the consistency of the hummus. Thin
out the hummus with some of the reserved chick
pea liquid, or more yogurt or oil if preferred,
to obtain a smooth consistency. Taste, and
adjust seasonings.

4 If serving hummus in pepper cups, cut off the
stalk ends of the peppers, halve the peppers
crossways, and scoop out the cores and seeds.
Fill with hummus and garnish as desired.

Cooking tip: Dried chick peas must always be soaked before
cooking. Soak in water to cover by 5 cm (2 in) for at least
8 hours, or overnight. If you are short of time, use the quick-
soak method: place the chick peas in a large saucepan and add
enough water to cover by 2.5 cm (1 in). Bring to a boil,
reduce the heat, and simmer for 2 minutes. Remove from the
heat and let stand, tightly covered, for 1 hour.
Whichever method you use, discard the soaking water, and
rinse and cook the chick peas in fresh water for 1 1/2–2 hours.

BABA GHANOUSH

This garlicky, lemony aubergine dip from the Middle East
will have a deeper roasted flavour if you include some – or
all – of the charred skin of the baked aubergines.
Serves 10–12

INGREDIENTS

1 kg (2 lb) aubergines
juice of 1 lemon, more to taste
2 garlic cloves, finely chopped or crushed
2 tbsp olive oil
2 tbsp plain low-fat yogurt
2 tbsp sesame tahini
1/4–1/2 tsp ground cumin
salt and freshly ground pepper

PREPARATION

1 Cut the aubergines in half lengthways, and score
the cut sides with a sharp knife down to the skin,
but not through it.

2 Place the aubergine halves, cut-side down, on an
oiled baking tray. Bake in a preheated 230°C
(450°F, Gas 8) oven for 20–30 minutes, until the
skin is charred and shrivelled. Remove from the
oven and let cool.

3 If you like the charred taste, leave the skin on the
aubergines; otherwise remove it. Discard any
seeds from the aubergines. Blend together the
aubergines, lemon juice, garlic, oil, yogurt,
tahini, and cumin to taste in a food processor
fitted with the metal blade. Add salt and pepper
to taste, and more lemon juice if you prefer.

BAGNA CAUDA

The Italian dip, Bagna Cauda, *literally means "hot bath".*
Traditionally it is served in an earthenware pot (see
page 31), also called a bagna cauda, *that has its own small*
burner. You could use a fondue set or warming plate instead.
Serves 4

INGREDIENTS

1 small head of celery
1 cucumber
1 large red pepper
250 g (8 oz) baby aubergines
250 ml (8 fl oz) olive oil
45 g (1 1/2 oz) unsalted butter
3–5 large garlic cloves, finely chopped
8 anchovy fillets, rinsed thoroughly, patted
dry, and chopped
salt (optional)
1/2 ciabatta loaf, sliced

Bagna cauda

Ciabatta slices

WARM DIP
Celery stalks, cucumber wedges, grilled red pepper strips and
aubergine quarters, and sliced ciabatta bread accompany
Bagna Cauda.

Dipping vegetables

PREPARATION

1 Wash the celery, and break it up into individual stalks. Cut the cucumber into long wedges. Core, seed, and cut the red pepper into eighths. Cut the aubergines lengthways into quarters.

2 Brush the red pepper and aubergine with some olive oil. Place under a medium-hot preheated grill for 3–5 minutes and cook, turning often, until lightly browned. Set the vegetables aside.

3 Melt the butter in a heavy-based saucepan over low heat. Add garlic to taste, and cook until it softens. Do not let it colour at all.

4 Stir in the anchovies, then slowly add the remaining olive oil in a thin stream, stirring and mashing the anchovies constantly with a wooden spoon. When all of the oil has been added, the anchovies should have dissolved into a paste. Taste, and add salt if you prefer.

5 Pour the dip into a *bagna cauda* or other flame-proof pot set over a burner or candle. Serve immediately while the dip is still hot, with the vegetables and ciabatta slices for dipping.

AÏOLI PLATTER

This is a traditional Provençal dish consisting of a garlic-flavoured mayonnaise dip with lightly cooked vegetables for dipping. I like to introduce other distinctively flavoured dips to diversify the platter. I usually steam or blanch the vegetables until just crisp-tender because they are easy to handle this way, but I also add a few uncooked red peppers and cherry tomatoes to give some bright, fresh colour. There is sometimes fish on an aïoli platter. Here I have used prawns; they are not traditional but they make the best finger food.

TO MAKE AN AÏOLI PLATTER

Serves 15

INGREDIENTS

500 g (1 lb) new potatoes
500 g (1 lb) baby carrots, peeled, with green tops left on
375 g (12 oz) green beans, trimmed
375 g (12 oz) green asparagus, trimmed
125 g (4 oz) baby sweetcorn
4 baby artichokes
375 g (12 oz) cherry tomatoes
1 large or 2 medium red peppers, cored, seeded, and cut into wide strips
500 g (1 lb) cooked medium prawns, peeled, with the tails left on
2 or 3 Aïoli Dips (see page 34)

PREPARATION

1 Steam or boil the potatoes until just tender. Let cool, then cut into halves or quarters. Steam or blanch the carrots, green beans, asparagus, baby sweetcorn, and artichokes until just tender. Halve the artichokes lengthways.

2 Arrange the cooked vegetables, the cherry tomatoes, pepper strips, and prawns on a platter with the aïoli dips in the centre.

All the vegetables can be prepared and cooked a day in advance and kept in covered containers in the refrigerator.

CRUNCHY DIPPERS & SPICY DIPS
Centre stage of an Aïoli Platter are (clockwise, from top) Sun-dried Tomato Aïoli, Chipotle Aïoli, and the classic Aïoli.

AIOLI DIPS

Aïoli is a pungent garlic mayonnaise. Sun-dried tomatoes add extra flavour and a reddish hue,
while chipotle – smoked jalapeño peppers – add piquancy.
Make aïoli as mild or as strong as you prefer by varying the amount of garlic.

★

AIOLI

Aïoli will keep up to a day in the refrigerator but it is best
made on the day you wish to serve it.
Makes about 350 ml (12 fl oz)

INGREDIENTS

3–6 large garlic cloves, total weight 15–30 g
(1/2–1 oz), peeled and cut in half lengthways,
bitter cores removed
salt and freshly ground pepper
1 small potato, cooked, mashed, and sieved (optional)
2 large egg yolks
350 ml (12 fl oz) olive oil
1 tbsp lemon juice (optional)

PREPARATION

1 Pound the garlic in a pestle and mortar with
1/2 tsp salt until smooth. Mix in the mashed
potato, if using.
2 Beat the egg yolks at high speed in an electric
mixer fitted with the balloon whisk or egg
beaters, until smooth.
3 Add the oil, a few drops at a time, and continue
to beat at high speed. Add half of the oil in this
way, then add the remainder in a very slow,
thin stream, or 1 tbsp at a time. The mayonnaise
will be very thick. When all of the oil has been
added, mix in the garlic at low speed.
4 Transfer to a bowl, taste, and stir in lemon
juice and pepper if you prefer.

VARIATION

INSTANT AIOLI: Stir the pounded garlic into
350 ml (12 fl oz) bottled mayonnaise. Omit the
potato, and add *2 tbsp olive oil* for flavour.

Food processor method

After completing step 1, break 1 whole egg instead of 2 egg
yolks into the bowl of a food processor fitted with the metal
blade. With the food processor running, slowly add the oil
in a very thin stream, or drop by drop. When all of the oil
has been added, work in the crushed garlic.

SUN-DRIED TOMATO AIOLI

Makes about 350 ml (12 fl oz)

INGREDIENTS

3 large garlic cloves, peeled and cut in half lengthways,
bitter cores removed
salt and freshly ground pepper
1 small potato, cooked, mashed, and sieved (optional)
2 large egg yolks
350 ml (12 fl oz) olive oil
1 tbsp lemon juice (optional)
4–5 oil-packed sun-dried tomatoes, rinsed and chopped

PREPARATION

1 Pound the garlic in a pestle and mortar with
1/2 tsp salt until smooth. Mix in the mashed
potato, if using.
2 Beat the egg yolks at high speed in an electric
mixer fitted with the balloon whisk or egg
beaters, until smooth.
3 Add the oil, a few drops at a time, and continue
to beat at high speed. Add half of the oil in this
way, then add the remainder in a very slow,
thin stream, or 1 tbsp at a time. The mayonnaise
will be very thick. When all of the oil has been
added, mix in the garlic at low speed.
4 Transfer to a bowl, taste, and stir in lemon
juice and pepper if you prefer.
5 Transfer half of the aïoli to another bowl and
set aside. Work in the sun-dried tomatoes. Stir
this mixture into the plain aïoli.

VARIATIONS

CHIPOTLE AIOLI: Substitute *1–2 canned chipotle*
chillies, drained, cored, seeded, and chopped, for the
sun-dried tomatoes.
LOW-FAT SUN-DRIED TOMATO OR CHIPOTLE
AIOLI: Substitute *175 ml (6 fl oz) low-fat fromage*
blanc or yogurt for half of the aïoli.

EGGS & CHEESE

Here is a wide range of colourful frittatas, piquant
devilled eggs, elegant little blini, and festive gougères
and crêpes. You'll find the frittatas incredibly easy
to make, and they look so good. I love making blini
the focus of a party table, especially when topped
with smoked salmon and fromage blanc. As I often
have to prepare in advance for a party, dishes such as
frittatas, blini, and crêpes are ideal, because they
can all be made well in advance.

FRITTATAS

Almost every time I entertain, I make frittatas – flat Italian omelettes. They look beautiful on a party table, when cut into diamond shapes. Make them a day ahead and keep them in the refrigerator, stacked in pairs. Cut them just before serving. You can add chopped fresh herbs, any type of vegetable, seafood, and meat to the basic frittata recipe below, or use the fillings on pages 38 and 39.

Parsley

TO MAKE A FRITTATA

Makes 60 x 3.5-cm (1½-in) diamond shapes

1 Beat together 10 large eggs and 3 tbsp milk with salt and freshly ground pepper to taste.

2 Prepare your choice of filling, and stir in.

3 Heat 1 tbsp olive oil in a 30-cm (12-in) non-stick frying pan over medium-high heat. Pour in the egg mixture and stir with a fork.

4 Shake the pan gently, lifting up the edge of the frittata to let the egg mixture run underneath. Reduce the heat to low, cover, and cook for about 10 minutes. The eggs should be just set.

5 Brown the top of the frittata under a preheated grill for about 2 minutes. Let cool.

BRIGHT & SAVOURY DIAMONDS
Courgette & Red Pepper Frittata (left and right on platter) flank Tender Pea & Pepper Frittata (above) and Smoked Salmon & Dill Frittata (below).

Black pepper

Salt

Courgette

Red pepper

SERVING A FRITTATA

Onion

1 Loosen the edge of the frittata from the pan with a palette knife. Slide the frittata out of the pan.

2 Cut the frittata into diamond-shaped pieces, and arrange in a decorative pattern on a serving platter.

Garlic

Milk

Beaten egg

FRITTATA FILLINGS

Frittatas make an ideal base for any number of fillings. Depending on the ingredients used, they can encompass a wide range of flavours — the choice is all yours. Colourful and tasty ingredients are essential, so try to mix and match for best effect.

★

COURGETTE & RED PEPPER

For a 30-cm (12-in) frittata

INGREDIENTS

1–2 tbsp olive oil
1 large onion, chopped
1 large red pepper, cored, seeded, and diced
750 g (1 1/2 lb) courgettes, scrubbed and diced
2 large garlic cloves, finely chopped or crushed
salt and freshly ground pepper
3 tbsp chopped fresh parsley,
or a mixture of parsley and other herbs,
such as basil, chives, tarragon, and chervil

PREPARATION

1 Heat 1 tbsp oil in a large, heavy-based non-stick frying pan over medium heat. Add the chopped onion, and cook for about 3 minutes, stirring often, until it begins to soften.
2 Add the red pepper, and cook, stirring, for a few minutes, until the pepper begins to soften.
3 Add the courgettes and garlic with salt and pepper to taste. Add 1 tbsp more oil, if necessary, or 2 tbsp water.
4 Cook for 5–10 minutes, stirring, until the courgettes are tender but still bright green.
5 Stir in the chopped herbs.

VARIATION

GREEN & RED PEPPER FRITTATA: Substitute *2 large green peppers* for the courgettes and add *1 more red pepper*. For a sweeter taste, roast the peppers.

SPINACH & FRESH HERB

For a 30-cm (12-in) frittata

INGREDIENTS

500 g (1 lb) spinach, stalks removed, leaves washed
salt
leaves from 1 large bunch of flat-leaf parsley, chopped
30 g (1 oz) mixed fresh herbs, such as mint, chervil, chives,
basil, and tarragon, chopped
2–3 large garlic cloves, finely chopped or crushed

PREPARATION

1 Blanch the spinach in a large pan of boiling salted water for 1–2 minutes. Alternatively, put the spinach in a dry non-stick frying pan with only the water left on the leaves after washing. Toss over high heat for 1–2 minutes until wilted.
2 Rinse the spinach under cold water, squeeze dry in a tea towel, and chop.
3 Combine the spinach with the herbs and garlic.

SMOKED SALMON & DILL

For a 30-cm (12-in) frittata

INGREDIENTS

1 tbsp olive oil
1 onion, chopped
375 g (12 oz) smoked salmon, diced
3 tbsp chopped fresh dill

PREPARATION

1 Heat the oil in a heavy-based non-stick frying pan over medium heat. Add the chopped onion, and cook about 5 minutes, stirring often, until tender.
2 Remove from the heat and stir in the diced salmon and dill.

Smoked Salmon & Dill Frittata

GINGER, BEAN SPROUT, & CORIANDER

For a 30-cm (12-in) frittata

INGREDIENTS

1 tbsp sunflower or rapeseed oil
2 bunches of spring onions, both white and
green parts, thinly sliced
1 large red pepper, cored,
seeded, and diced
1-cm (1/2-in) piece of fresh root ginger,
peeled and finely chopped or crushed
2 large garlic cloves, finely chopped or crushed
250 g (8 oz) bean sprouts, trimmed
and coarsely chopped
2–3 tsp soy sauce
60 g (2 oz) fresh coriander, chopped
salt and freshly ground pepper

PREPARATION

1 Heat the oil in a large, heavy-based non-stick
frying pan over medium heat. Add the spring
onions and red pepper, and cook for 1–2 minutes,
stirring constantly, until the vegetables begin
to soften.
2 Add the ginger, garlic, and bean sprouts. Cook
for about 1 minute, stirring.
3 Drain off and discard any liquid which may have
accumulated in the pan.
4 Stir the soy sauce into the vegetables and remove
the pan from the heat. Stir in the chopped
coriander.
5 Taste, and adjust seasonings, adding more soy
sauce or salt, and pepper to taste.

FRITTATA FACTS

- *Frittatas can be made in any sized frying pan: the only*
  requirement is that the pan should be heavy-based in
  order to transmit and retain the heat and so produce an
  evenly cooked frittata. A non-stick coating also helps.

- *Frittatas are cooked differently from omelettes, which are*
  cooked very quickly over high heat, whereas frittatas
  require slow cooking over low heat.

- *While omelettes should be moist and creamy, the perfect*
  frittata is set and firm, without being dry.

- *Omelettes are served folded over, but a frittata takes on*
  the shape of the pan in which it has been cooked.

ASPARAGUS

For a 30-cm (12-in) frittata

INGREDIENTS

500 g (1 lb) green asparagus, trimmed and cut
into 1-cm (1/2-in) lengths
3 tbsp chopped fresh chives

PREPARATION

Steam the asparagus for about 8 minutes, until
tender and still bright green. Drain and rinse
under cold water. Shake dry. Combine with the
chopped chives.

TENDER PEA & PEPPER

For a 30-cm (12-in) frittata

INGREDIENTS

1 tbsp olive oil
1 medium onion, chopped
1 large red pepper, cored, seeded, and diced
salt and freshly ground pepper
2 large garlic cloves, finely chopped or crushed
750 g (11/2 lb) fresh peas (unshelled weight), shelled,
or 375 g (12 oz) frozen peas

PREPARATION

1 Heat the oil in a large, heavy-based non-stick
frying pan over medium heat. Add the onion,
and cook for about 3 minutes, stirring, until it
begins to soften.
2 Add the red pepper and a little salt, and stir
together well. Cook, stirring often, until just
tender, 5 minutes.
3 Stir in the garlic, cook for 1 minute, then
remove the mixture from the heat.
4 If using fresh peas, steam them for 5–8 minutes,
until tender, then rinse under cold water. Defrost
frozen peas by dropping them into boiling water
for 2 minutes, and then draining them.
5 Stir the peas into the onion and pepper mixture,
with salt and pepper to taste.

DEVILLED EGGS

Hard-boiled egg-white halves make perfect containers for yolks speckled with freshly chopped herbs, enriched with tuna, or filled with pungent Provençal olives, capers, and anchovies. Mustard is used to pep up most of these fillings, although many other piquant flavourings are included. The eggs can be boiled and the fillings (minus lemon juice, if among the ingredients) made a day ahead and refrigerated. Do not, however, fill and assemble the eggs more than an hour before serving or the filling may discolour and separate.

LITTLE DEVILS

Herb Pot Pourri filling is piped into hard-boiled egg halves and topped with salami and herb garnish (around platter). On the platter, Tapenade-filled egg coronets, garnished with parsley, are surrounded by eggs filled with piped Smoked Trout filling and garnished with smoked salmon diamonds and lemon zest.

**Herb Pot Pourri
Devilled Eggs**

TO MAKE DEVILLED EGGS

Makes 24

1 Put 12 large eggs in a saucepan with water to cover. Bring to a boil over medium-high heat, reduce the heat, and simmer for 10 minutes.

2 Remove the eggs from the heat and run under cold water for several minutes until the eggs have cooled down.

3 Peel the eggs, and cut lengthways in half or, if you prefer, shape the eggs into coronets as directed on page 43.

4 Remove the yolks and use, where indicated, in the fillings given on pages 42–43.

5 Pipe or spoon the fillings into the egg-white halves. Garnish if you prefer.

DEVILLED EGG FILLINGS

Savoury ingredients, often combined with the yolks from hard-boiled eggs, make delicious fillings for egg-white halves.

★

HERB POT POURRI

Use any combination of fresh herbs for this green- and yellow-speckled filling.
Add the lemon juice just before you fill the eggs —
it will discolour the herbs if added too soon.
For 24 Devilled Eggs

INGREDIENTS

yolks from 12 hard-boiled eggs
4 tbsp plain low-fat yogurt
3 tbsp mayonnaise
2 tsp Dijon mustard
1–2 tbsp lemon juice
30 g (1 oz) fresh herbs, such as parsley, tarragon, chervil, chives, thyme, dill, marjoram, and basil, finely chopped
salt and freshly ground pepper

PREPARATION

1 In a food processor fitted with the metal blade, or in a pestle and mortar, blend together the egg yolks, yogurt, mayonnaise, mustard, and lemon juice to taste until smooth (this can also be done by pressing the ingredients through a fine sieve).
2 Stir in the chopped mixed herbs, with salt and pepper to taste.

SMOKED TROUT

For 24 Devilled Eggs

INGREDIENTS

yolks from 6 hard-boiled eggs
(reserve remaining yolks for another use)
250 g (8 oz) smoked trout fillets
6 tbsp plain low-fat yogurt or fromage blanc (see page 156)
2–3 tbsp lemon juice
2 tsp Dijon mustard
salt and freshly ground pepper

PREPARATION

Work the egg yolks with the trout in a food processor fitted with the metal blade. Add the yogurt, lemon juice to taste, and mustard, and work again. Add salt and pepper to taste.

CURRIED KEDGEREE

Kedgeree, a smoked haddock rice dish invented during the British occupation of India, is traditionally garnished with hard-boiled eggs. In this recipe, the roles have been reversed.
For 24 Devilled Eggs

INGREDIENTS

60 g (2 oz) butter
1 small onion, finely chopped
125 g (4 oz) long-grain rice
2 tsp mild curry paste or powder
1/4 tsp turmeric
250 ml (8 fl oz) milk and water mixed, for poaching
200 g (7 oz) smoked haddock fillets
2 tbsp plain low-fat yogurt or soured cream
yolks from 6 hard-boiled eggs
(reserve remaining yolks for another use)
1 tbsp chopped fresh parsley
salt and freshly ground pepper

PREPARATION

1 Melt the butter in a saucepan, add the onion, and fry gently until soft. Add the rice and, when it is transparent, add the curry paste or powder and turmeric. Pour in enough water to cover, and simmer over low heat for about 15 minutes, or until the rice is tender. Drain and let cool.
2 Bring the milk and water mixture to a boil, add the smoked haddock, and poach over low heat for 10 minutes. Remove and discard all the skin and bones from the smoked haddock, and break up the flesh into very small pieces. Let cool.
3 In a large bowl, mix the curried rice, smoked haddock, yogurt or soured cream, egg yolks, and parsley until well combined. Season the mixture with salt and pepper.

TAPENADE

Tapenade, the pungent Provençal paste, is extremely versatile, serving not only as a filling for Devilled Eggs, but also as a topping for Bruschetta and Crostini, and a stuffing for vegetables. Tapenade will keep for up to a week in the refrigerator.
For 24 Devilled Eggs

INGREDIENTS

2 large garlic cloves
1 1/2 tbsp capers, drained and rinsed
4 anchovy fillets, rinsed
1 tsp fresh thyme leaves,
or 1/2 tsp dried thyme
1 tsp chopped fresh rosemary,
or 1/2 tsp crumbled dried rosemary
2 tbsp lemon juice
2 tbsp olive oil
1 tsp Dijon mustard
freshly ground black pepper
yolks from 6 hard-boiled eggs
(reserve remaining yolks for another use)
250 g (8 oz) black olives, stoned and coarsely chopped

PREPARATION

1 Turn on a food processor fitted with the metal blade, and drop in the garlic. When it is chopped, turn off the machine and add the capers, anchovies, thyme, and rosemary. Process until fairly smooth.
2 Add the lemon juice, olive oil, mustard, and black pepper to taste, and process again.
3 Add the egg yolks and work again, until the mixture is smooth. Turn the mixture into a bowl and beat in the chopped olives.

EGG SHAPES

- *For well-centred yolks, use only fresh eggs. The older an egg, the larger the air pocket inside. The yolk will travel towards this when the egg rests in the pan during boiling, resulting in a lopsided yolk cavity in the boiled egg.*

- *To make egg coronets, make a small angled cut with the tip of a small knife in the middle of a hard-boiled egg. Remove the knife and make another cut in the opposite direction to meet a tip of the first cut. Continue around the egg and pull the halves apart. Remove the yolk.*

- *Once you have halved the eggs, cut a small slice off the base of each half so that it does not topple over.*

CHICKEN, AVOCADO, & SWEETCORN

This filling is made without hard-boiled egg yolks.
For 24 Devilled Eggs

INGREDIENTS

250 g (8 oz) cooked chicken, shredded
1 large avocado, stoned, peeled, and finely diced
cooked kernels from 2 ears of sweetcorn
6 tbsp lime juice
1 large tomato, finely chopped
2 fresh green chillies, cored, seeded, and finely chopped
6 tbsp chopped fresh coriander
salt and freshly ground pepper

PREPARATION

Toss together all the ingredients, with salt and pepper to taste.

Garnish suggestion: *Reserve any hard-boiled yolks not used in the recipe to use as a garnish. Press through a sieve, then sprinkle over the filled eggs or other party fare, such as Blini (see pages 46–47) or Nachos (see pages 82–83).*

TUNA

Tuna flavoured with lemon juice makes a tangy and refreshing filling. This is a recipe you can put together at any time from staples in your kitchen.
For 24 Devilled Eggs

INGREDIENTS

375 g (12 oz) water-packed tuna, drained
yolks from 12 hard-boiled eggs
2 tbsp olive oil
125 ml (4 fl oz) plain low-fat yogurt
1 tsp Dijon mustard
1–2 large garlic cloves, finely chopped or crushed
1–2 tbsp lemon juice
salt and freshly ground pepper

PREPARATION

1 Using a fork, flake the tuna until it is quite smooth. Add the egg yolks, olive oil, yogurt, and mustard, and mix together until fairly smooth.
2 Add garlic, lemon juice, salt, and pepper to taste, and mix well together.

BLINI WITH SAVOURY TOPPINGS

Plump little pancakes, blini are among my favourite party foods. They make marvellous vehicles for a wide variety of toppings, from luxurious ingredients such as smoked salmon and caviar to salsa and sweetcorn, radishes, onions, capers and chopped eggs – you can be as creative as you like. A combination of dark buckwheat and light cornmeal blini provides an attractive contrast, both in colour and flavour. You can make blini well in advance and freeze them: they can be easily heated from frozen and quickly assembled.

BLOND BLINI

Cornmeal blini are an American variation on the traditional Russian buckwheat blini. They are an ideal base for piquant toppings such as Corn & Tomato Salsa and Cream Cheese & Radish Rose.

Corn & Tomato Salsa Blini

Cream Cheese & Radish Rose Blini

BROWN BLINI

Buckwheat blini make mouthwatering savoury finger foods when topped with a range of fish and meats, such as Smoked Salmon & Fromage Blanc, Caviar & Fromage Blanc, and Smoked Turkey & Mustard.

Smoked Turkey & Mustard Blini

Smoked Salmon & Fromage Blanc Blini

TO MAKE TOPPED BLINI

Makes 50

1 Make the blini as directed on page 146.

2 To prevent the blini becoming soggy, overlap rather than stack them on a plate when you transfer them from the pan. If you are not serving them immediately, the blini can be wrapped in a tea towel or foil. Reheat, wrapped in foil, in a preheated 160°C (325°F, Gas 3) oven for 30 minutes.

3 Prepare your choice of toppings from the recipes given on pages 46–47. Spoon, spread, or pipe on to the blini, and serve the blini as warm as possible.

You can make blini in advance and freeze them. Stack them interleaved with parchment paper and wrap tightly in foil, then seal in a plastic bag. To defrost the blini, remove them from the plastic bag and heat the foil packet in a preheated 180°C (350°F, Gas 4) oven for 1 hour.

Caviar & Fromage Blanc Blini

INTERNATIONAL BLINI

Blini are small, light pancakes made with yeast, and are part of the Russian tradition of zakuski, the ever-ready array of snacks and hors d'oeuvre. The batter for Russian blini is made from a mixture of buckwheat and white flours. Buckwheat is an easy grain to grow, because it does not require fertile soil. Originally, blini had a religious significance: they were eaten during the festivities of "butter week", the final days of the carnival that preceded and anticipated the abstinence and austerity of Lent. Today, wherever they are eaten, the Russian tradition

lingers on, because blini are typically served with caviar, and smoked salmon or herring and soured cream, usually as snacks for visitors, or as appetizers, with ice-cold vodka to complement their richness.

Cornmeal blini, an American invention, are lighter and more colourful than buckwheat blini, while French blini are made with white flour only. In France, blini can be bought ready made at charcuteries to accompany the smoked salmon that is usually sold there.

BLINI TOPPINGS

A layer of fromage blanc, a sliver of smoked salmon, a wisp of dill, a few luxurious beads of caviar, these are just a few of the many ingredients that can make stunning toppings for blini. You can follow my suggestions to the letter, or mix and match to create combinations of your own.

★

SMOKED TURKEY & MUSTARD

This topping has only two ingredients; it is delicious served on earthy-flavoured buckwheat blini.
For 50 blini

INGREDIENTS

250 g (8 oz) smoked turkey, thinly sliced
6 tbsp Dijon mustard

PREPARATION

1 Cut the smoked turkey into 50 small diamond or other shapes, using a small pastry cutter or aspic cutter for a neat finish.
2 Spread a little Dijon mustard thinly and evenly on top of each blini and top with a piece of smoked turkey.

SMOKED SALMON & FROMAGE BLANC

For 50 blini

INGREDIENTS

about 150 ml (¼ pint) fromage blanc or drained yogurt
(see page 156)
about 375 g (12 oz) smoked salmon, thinly sliced
freshly ground pepper

PREPARATION

1 Spread about 1 heaped tsp fromage blanc or yogurt on each blini.
2 Cut the smoked salmon to fit the tops of the blini and place on top of the fromage blanc or yogurt. Sprinkle the salmon with pepper to taste.

CAVIAR & FROMAGE BLANC

Beluga caviar is superb on blini, but you can also use salmon caviar. If you are using fine caviar, don't mix it into the fromage blanc or yogurt mixture.
For 50 blini

INGREDIENTS

350 ml (12 fl oz) fromage blanc or drained yogurt
(see page 156)
2 hard-boiled eggs, finely chopped
1 small red onion, finely chopped
60 g (2 oz) caviar
freshly ground pepper

PREPARATION

1 Mix together the fromage blanc or yogurt, the hard-boiled eggs, the onion, and the salmon caviar, if using. If using Beluga or other fine caviar, omit the yogurt and fromage blanc and do not mix in the caviar. Add pepper to taste.
2 Top each blini with 1 heaped tsp of the mixture. If using fine caviar, top each blini with the egg and onion mixture, then place ½ tsp caviar on top.

GOLDEN EGGS

Caviar is matured sturgeon's roe that has been salted to preserve it. It is expensive because sturgeon is rare and the female fish must be over 15 years old before the roe can be made into caviar. Caviar comes chiefly from Russia and Iran, and is graded into three types, according to the species of sturgeon, the colour of the eggs, and egg size.
Beluga, *the rarest and most expensive of caviars, comes from the largest species of sturgeon. The eggs are large and very fragile, and their colour varies from pale to dark grey.*
Osetra *is prized for its distinctive nutty flavour. The rich golden brown eggs are smaller than Beluga.*
Sevruga *is small and fine-grained, and varies in colour from light to dark grey.*

CORN & TOMATO SALSA

This salsa is colourful and spicy, with contrasting textures
as well as sweet and pungent flavours.
For 50 blini

INGREDIENTS

kernels from 1 ear of sweetcorn
500 g (1 lb) ripe tomatoes, finely chopped
1/2 small red onion, finely chopped
1–3 fresh green chillies, cored, seeded,
and finely chopped
4 tbsp chopped fresh coriander
1 tbsp balsamic vinegar
salt

PREPARATION

1 Steam the corn kernels for about 5 minutes,
until barely tender and quite juicy. Remove
from the heat and rinse under cold water.
2 Mix together the tomatoes, onion, chillies to
taste, coriander, vinegar, and salt to taste.
3 Top each blini with the salsa, then with the corn,
or mix the salsa and corn together, if you prefer.

Quick Blini Toppings

To put together a few topped blini quickly, try these easy
combinations:

CREAM CHEESE & RADISH ROSE: Put *1 heaped tsp cream*
cheese on each blini. Stuff *prepared radish roses (see page*
149) with *cream cheese combined with diced tomatillo,* and
place one rose on each topped blini. Garnish with
chopped chives.

RICOTTA CHEESE & RED PEPPER: Chop or thinly slice
ready-grilled red peppers, then toss the slices with *finely*
chopped or crushed garlic and *balsamic vinegar.* Put about
1 tsp ricotta cheese on each blini, then top with the red
pepper mixture, and garnish with *slivered fresh basil.*

GREEN TOMATILLO SALSA

For 50 blini

INGREDIENTS

250 g (8 oz) tomatillos, husked,
or 1 x 400-g (14-oz) can tomatillos, drained
2–3 fresh green chillies, cored and seeded
1/2 medium onion, roughly chopped
2 large garlic cloves, roughly chopped (optional)
6 sprigs of fresh coriander
salt
125 ml (4 fl oz) fromage blanc (see page 156),
plain low-fat yogurt, or soured cream

PREPARATION

1 If using fresh tomatillos, put in a pan with water
to cover and simmer for 10 minutes, then drain.
2 Process the cooked or canned tomatillos with
chillies to taste, the onion, garlic if using, and the
coriander sprigs to a coarse purée in a blender
or a food processor fitted with the metal blade.
Season with salt to taste, and let stand for
30 minutes or longer before serving.
3 Top each blini with 1 tsp of the salsa, and about
1/2 tsp fromage blanc, yogurt, or soured cream.

MANGO SALSA

For 50 blini

INGREDIENTS

1 ripe mango, peeled and finely chopped
2 small fresh green chillies, cored, seeded, and chopped
1 tbsp chopped fresh coriander
4 tbsp prepared Tomato Salsa (see page 29)
juice of 1 medium lime

PREPARATION

1 Toss together all the ingredients and let stand in
a cool place for 1 hour.
2 Distribute the salsa evenly on top of the blini.

Cream Cheese & Radish Rose Blini

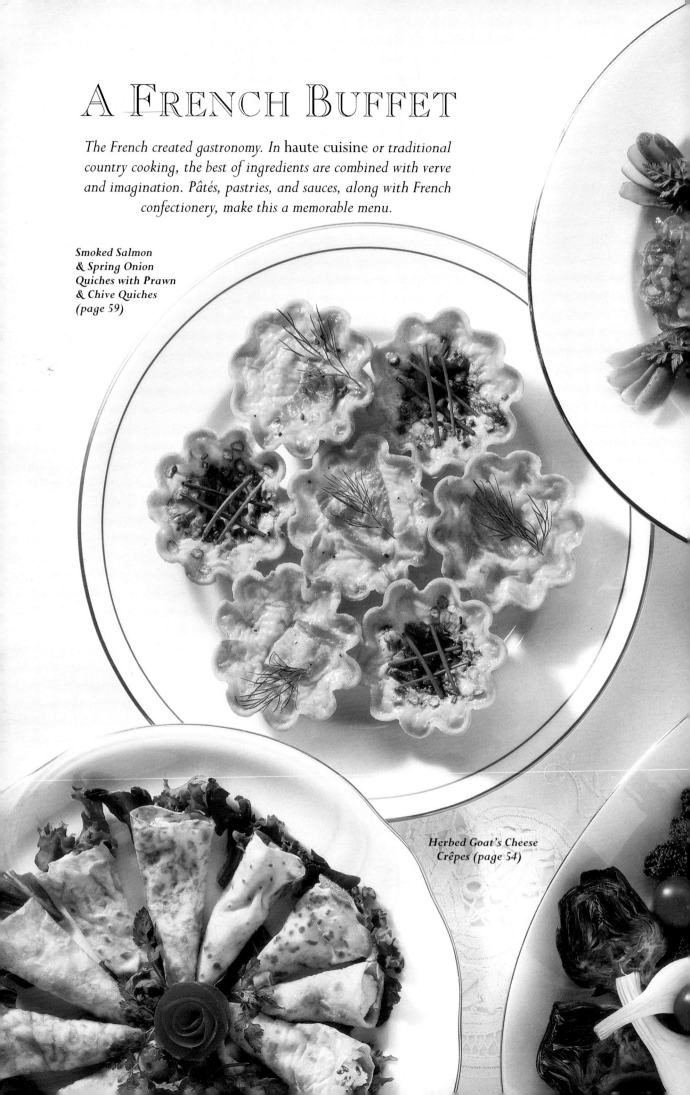

A French Buffet

The French created gastronomy. In haute cuisine or traditional country cooking, the best of ingredients are combined with verve and imagination. Pâtés, pastries, and sauces, along with French confectionery, make this a memorable menu.

Smoked Salmon & Spring Onion Quiches with Prawn & Chive Quiches *(page 59)*

Herbed Goat's Cheese Crêpes (page 54)

Lamb Terrine en Gelée
(page 112) on canapés

Aïoli Platter (page 32)

Creamy Chocolate & Orange
Bouchées (page 125)

Lemon Sablés
(page 127)

GOUGÈRES

Usually made in large rings, gougères are savoury choux pastries. To serve as finger food, I make bite-sized pastries. Traditionally, they are made with Gruyère or Emmental cheese, so if you wish to keep with tradition, add 60 g (2 oz) grated cheese to the basic recipe on page 138.

★

BLUE CHEESE & PEAR GOUGÈRES

Makes 40

INGREDIENTS

*125 ml (4 fl oz) fromage blanc (see page 156),
or 6 tbsp low-fat cottage cheese and 2 tbsp plain low-fat yogurt
175 g (6 oz) blue cheese, roughly chopped
1 large ripe pear, peeled, cored, and finely chopped
30 g (1 oz) blanched almonds, finely chopped
freshly ground pepper
40 bite-sized gougères (see page 138), baked and cooled*

PREPARATION

1 If using fromage blanc, work together with the blue cheese in a food processor fitted with the metal blade, until smooth.
2 If using the cottage cheese and yogurt mixture, work them together first until smooth, then add the blue cheese and work again until smooth.
3 Stir in the chopped pear and almonds. Mix well, and add pepper to taste.
4 Cut the tops off the gougères, and reserve for lids. Divide the filling evenly among the gougères, and replace the tops.

GOAT'S CHEESE & PEPPER GOUGÈRES

Makes 40

INGREDIENTS

*2 red peppers
375 g (12 oz) goat's cheese
2 garlic cloves, roughly chopped
2–4 tbsp plain low-fat yogurt
salt and freshly ground pepper
40 bite-sized gougères (see page 138),
baked and cooled*

PREPARATION

1 Grill the peppers until the skins are evenly charred, then seal in a plastic bag or place in a covered bowl until cool.
2 Skin, core, and seed the grilled peppers. Purée the peppers in a food processor fitted with the metal blade. Add the goat's cheese and garlic and blend together. Add enough yogurt to thin out as desired. Add salt and pepper to taste.
3 Cut the tops off the gougères, and reserve for lids. Divide the filling evenly among the gougères, and replace the tops.

CHICKEN PROVENÇAL GOUGERES

The chicken filling in these gougères tastes very good in cheese-flavoured pastry. You can also use other light meats, such as poultry, pork, or veal, and blend them with robust Mediterranean ingredients to create strongly flavoured, satisfying gougères.
Makes 40

INGREDIENTS

250 g (8 oz) spinach, leaves washed, stalks removed
salt and freshly ground pepper
300 g (10 oz) shredded cooked chicken, turkey, rabbit, pork, or veal, or a combination
2 tbsp olive oil
1 small onion, chopped
2 large garlic cloves, finely chopped or crushed
125 ml (4 fl oz) tomato sauce or passata
30 g (1 oz) fresh breadcrumbs
15 g (1/2 oz) fresh parsley, finely chopped
2 tbsp chopped fresh rosemary
2 tsp fresh thyme leaves, or 1 tsp dried thyme
40 bite-sized gougères (see page 138), baked and cooled

PREPARATION

1 Blanch the spinach in a large pan of boiling salted water for 1–2 minutes. Alternatively, put the spinach in a dry non-stick frying pan with only the water left on the leaves after washing. Toss over high heat for 1–2 minutes, until wilted.

2 Rinse the spinach under cold water, squeeze dry in a tea towel, and chop finely.

3 Chop the meat finely in a food processor. Add the spinach and mix together, using the pulse action of the food processor.

4 Heat the oil over medium heat in a heavy-based non-stick frying pan. Add the onion and cook for about 5 minutes, stirring, until tender. Add the garlic and cook together for 1 minute. Remove from the heat.

5 Add the onion and garlic to the meat and spinach mixture with the sauce, breadcrumbs, and herbs, adding salt and pepper to taste. Mix together well.

6 Cut the tops off the gougères, and reserve for lids. Divide the filling evenly among the gougères, and replace the tops.

MASHED POTATO & GARLIC GOUGERES

The reason for blanching the garlic several times is to make it sweeter and less pungent.
Makes 40

INGREDIENTS

2 large heads of garlic, cloves separated and peeled
3 litres (5 pints) water
salt and freshly ground pepper
500 g (1 lb) potatoes, peeled, cooked, mashed, and sieved
21/2 tbsp olive oil
40 bite-sized gougères (see page 138), baked and cooled

PREPARATION

1 Blanch the garlic: put the cloves and 1 litre (1¾ pints) of the water in a saucepan and bring to a boil. Pour off the water. Add half of the remaining water to the saucepan and bring to a boil. Pour off the water.

2 Add the remaining water and bring to a boil. Add 1 tsp salt, reduce the heat, and simmer for 30–40 minutes until the garlic is very tender and the liquid fragrant. Remove from the heat.

3 Using a slotted spoon or skimmer, transfer the garlic from the broth to a food processor fitted with the metal blade. Process until the garlic is thoroughly smooth.

4 Transfer the garlic to a large bowl and add the potatoes. Whisk or stir together until the mixture is well blended, then add the olive oil and 2 tbsp of the garlic broth. Add salt and pepper to taste.

5 Cut the tops off the gougères, and reserve for lids. Divide the filling evenly among the gougères, and replace the tops.

Freezing Gougères

Unfilled gougères freeze well. To defrost and crisp, place on a baking tray and heat through in a preheated 220°C (425°F, Gas 7) oven for 4 minutes.

CREPES

Elegant little crêpe triangles, stuffed with a variety of fillings, make terrific finger food. Their great advantage is that the crêpes themselves can be made well in advance and stored in the refrigerator. Heat as directed below before filling and serving.

★

MEXICAN-STYLE FISH CREPES

Makes 24

INGREDIENTS

12 peppercorns
1/4 tsp coriander seeds
1/4 tsp cinnamon or 5-mm (1/4-in) cinnamon stick
2 garlic cloves, peeled
1/2 tsp salt
2 tbsp water
2 tbsp sunflower or rapeseed oil
1/2 small white onion, chopped
2 fresh green chillies, cored, seeded, and finely chopped
250 g (8 oz) tomatoes, peeled and chopped
500 g (1 lb) fish fillets, such as shark,
mahi-mahi, or monkfish, cooked and shredded
12 crêpes (see page 147)

PREPARATION

1 Grind together the spices. Pound the garlic, using a pestle and mortar. Add the salt and ground spices. Grind together to a paste, then work in the water. The mixture should be smooth.
2 Heat the oil in a large heavy-based saucepan or non-stick frying pan over medium heat and add the onion. Cook, stirring, for about 3 minutes, until it begins to soften.
3 Add the chillies and tomatoes. Cook together, stirring constantly, for about 5 minutes. Stir in the garlic and ground spice mixture. Continue to cook together for 5 minutes.
4 Stir in the fish, mix together well, and cook, stirring, for 5 minutes. Remove from the heat, taste, and adjust seasonings.
5 Cut the crêpes in half. Warm them in a pan on top of the stove or in a preheated 180°C (350°F, Gas 4) oven. Fill and fold the crêpes as directed on page 53.
6 Arrange the crêpes on a serving platter, garnish as desired, and serve immediately.

ORIENTAL-STYLE CRAB CREPES

Makes 24

INGREDIENTS

250 g (8 oz) cooked white crabmeat, shredded
5 spring onions, both white and green parts, chopped
2 fresh hot green chillies (or 1 green and 1 red),
cored, seeded, and finely chopped
75 g (2½ oz) fresh coriander, chopped
4 tbsp sunflower or rapeseed oil
2 tbsp dark sesame oil
4 tbsp lime juice
1½ tsp soy sauce
2 tsp chopped or grated fresh root ginger
1 large garlic clove, finely chopped or crushed
salt
12 crêpes (see page 147)

FOR THE GARNISH (OPTIONAL)
24 peeled, cooked prawns
Tomato Rose (see page 154)
orange, lemon, and lime wedges
dill sprigs and basil leaves

PREPARATION

1 Toss together the crabmeat, spring onions, chillies, and coriander.
2 Stir together the sunflower or rapeseed and sesame oils with the lime juice, soy sauce, ginger, and garlic. Toss with the crab mixture. Add salt to taste.
3 Cut the crêpes in half. Warm them in a pan on top of the stove or in a preheated 180°C (350°F, Gas 4) oven. Fill and fold the crêpes as directed on page 53.
4 Arrange the crêpes on a serving platter, garnish as desired, and serve immediately.

CREPE FANTASY
Oriental-style Crab
Crêpes are garnished with
prawns, citrus wedges, herbs, and
a Tomato Rose (see page 154).

FILLING & FOLDING CREPES

1 Place about 1 tbsp filling in the centre of each crêpe half. Spread it out evenly over one side of the crêpe.

2 Lift the unfilled side of the crêpe, and fold it over the filling, until the two corners meet.

3 Fold the filled crêpe in half again, to make a small triangular parcel, with a little filling showing at the open end.

HERBED GOAT'S CHEESE CREPES

Makes 24

INGREDIENTS

375 g (12 oz) goat's cheese
90 ml (3 fl oz) plain low-fat yogurt
freshly ground pepper
2 tbsp chopped fresh parsley
12 crêpes (see page 147)

PREPARATION

1 Mash together the goat's cheese, yogurt, and pepper to taste. Stir in the parsley.
2 Cut the crêpes in half. Warm them in a pan on top of the stove or in a preheated 180°C (350°F, Gas 4) oven. Fill and fold the crêpes as directed on page 53.
3 Arrange the crêpes on a serving platter, garnish as desired, and serve immediately.

CHEESE & WILD MUSHROOM CREPES

Makes 24

INGREDIENTS

500 g (1 lb) wild mushrooms, such as ceps, girolles, morels, or oyster mushrooms (see page 156), stalks trimmed, thoroughly cleaned and dried, sliced 5-mm (1/4-in) thick
salt and freshly ground pepper
125 ml (4 fl oz) fruity red wine, such as a Côtes du Luberon, Gamay, or Beaujolais
1 tsp fresh thyme leaves, or 1/2 tsp dried thyme
1 tsp chopped fresh rosemary, or 1/2 tsp dried rosemary, crushed
2 tbsp olive oil
2 large garlic cloves, finely chopped or crushed
2 tbsp chopped fresh parsley
12 crêpes (see page 147)
125 g (4 oz) Gruyère cheese, grated

PREPARATION

1 Cook the mushrooms and salt over medium heat in a non-stick frying pan until they begin to release liquid. Cook, stirring, for 5 minutes or until the mushrooms just stick to the pan. Add the wine, thyme, and rosemary. Lower heat; simmer until wine is almost evaporated.
2 Add the olive oil, garlic, and pepper, and cook for about 5 minutes, stirring. Stir in the parsley and remove from the heat.

3 Cut the crêpes in half, sprinkle with grated Gruyère, and fill and fold as directed on page 53. Warm them in a preheated 190°C (375°F, Gas 5) oven for 10–15 minutes, until the cheese melts.
4 Arrange the crêpes on a serving platter, garnish as desired, and serve immediately.

PUMPKIN & ALMOND CREPES

The filling for these crêpes is traditionally used for making Tuscan tortellini.
Makes 24

INGREDIENTS

1 kg (2 lb) fresh pumpkin, seeds and membranes removed
175 ml (6 fl oz) fruity red wine, such as a Côtes du Luberon, Gamay, or Beaujolais
60 g (2 oz) almonds, skinned, toasted, and ground
60 g (2 oz) breadcrumbs, preferably wholewheat
2 tbsp chopped fresh sage, or 1 tsp dried sage
2 tsp mild honey, such as clover or acacia
1/2 tsp ground cinnamon
1/4–1/2 tsp ground nutmeg
salt and freshly ground pepper
60 g (2 oz) Parmesan cheese, freshly grated
12 crêpes (see page 147)

PREPARATION

1 Place the pumpkin in a lightly oiled baking dish, cover, and bake in a preheated 200°C (400°F, Gas 6) oven for 45 minutes, or until tender. Remove from the oven and let cool.
2 Cut away the rind from the pumpkin. Pour off any juice from the dish, and purée the flesh in a food processor fitted with the metal blade.
3 Combine the wine, almonds, breadcrumbs, sage, and honey in a large saucepan and bring to simmering point. Stir together until the wine has been absorbed and no more liquid remains in the pan.
4 Stir in the pumpkin and cinnamon. Add nutmeg, salt, and pepper to taste. Remove from the heat and stir in the Parmesan.
5 Cut the crêpes in half. Warm them in a pan on top of the stove or in a preheated 180°C (350°F, Gas 4) oven. Fill and fold the crêpes as directed on page 53.
6 Arrange the crêpes on a serving platter, garnish as desired, and serve immediately.

QUICHES &
SAVOURY BREADS

*This chapter offers the widest range of finger foods
and appetizers in this book. My passion for Italian
and Provençal food is evident here – you'll find robust
Mediterranean flavours throughout in quiches,
pizzas, calzone, focaccia, bruschetta, and crostini.
For the most part, they are easy to make, because
quiches, pizzas, and focaccia can be made
large, then cut into small pieces.*

QUICHES

Small and crisp quiches baked with delicious and appealing fillings are always a great hit on a party table. I have given a choice of pastry doughs for making the quiche shells. The Pâte Brisée can be made either by hand or in a food processor, and can be made in advance and frozen, if you prefer. The Yeasted Olive Oil Pastry is very light, and easy to make by hand.

Asparagus Quiche

TO MAKE QUICHES

Makes 8–10 x 7-cm (3-in) quiches

1 Choose your dough from the recipes given on pages 136–137.

2 Once you have made the dough, line the tins. Unless you are freezing the pastry shells, you should refrigerate them for 2 hours.

3 Prepare your choice of filling from the recipes given on pages 58–59.

4 Bake the pastry shells blind in a preheated 190°C (375°F, Gas 5) oven for 5 minutes.

5 Fill the pastry shells with the filling of your choice, then bake for 20 minutes or longer (see recipe), until the tops are just beginning to brown and the fillings have set.

Leek & Goat's Cheese Quiche

SAVOURY QUICHES

A tempting array of quiches offers a choice of fillings ranging from (around platter) Asparagus and Leek & Goat's Cheese to (on platter) Smoked Salmon & Spring Onion; Spinach; Courgette & Red Pepper; Wild Mushroom & Cheese; Prawn & Chive; Herb & Spring Onion; and Cherry Tomato & Basil.

Asparagus Quiche

TO MAKE & SERVE A LARGE QUICHE

• *If you want to make one large quiche instead of 8–10 small quiches, the quantity of dough in each of the recipes given on pages 136–137 will make one 25-cm (10-in) quiche. Each of the fillings given on pages 58–59 is enough for one large quiche.*

• *When you are ready to serve a large quiche, shape bite-sized portions in this simple and quick way: cut the quiche into 4-cm (1 1/2-in) strips, then turn and cut the strips on the diagonal to make small diamond-shaped pieces. Serve the pieces from the quiche tin, or arrange on a platter.*

Leek & Goat's Cheese Quiche

Asparagus Quiche

QUICHE FILLINGS

I use fresh, light ingredients for quiche fillings. When baked, the eggs and milk set to form a subtle base that highlights the contrasting flavours and textures of the other filling ingredients.

★

ASPARAGUS

*For 8–10 x 7-cm (3-in) quiches
or 1 x 25-cm (10-in) quiche*

INGREDIENTS

*500 g (1 lb) green asparagus, trimmed
1 bunch of spring onions,
both white and green parts, chopped
1 tbsp olive oil or butter
90 g (3 oz) Gruyère cheese, grated
30 g (1 oz) Parmesan cheese, grated
4 eggs, beaten
175 ml (6 fl oz) milk
salt and freshly ground pepper
1 tsp fresh thyme leaves*

PREPARATION

1 Steam the asparagus for 5 minutes, until just tender. Refresh the asparagus in cold water, and cut into 1-cm (1/2-in) lengths, reserving the tips for the garnish.

2 Cook the spring onions in the oil or butter for 3–5 minutes, stirring, until tender. Mix with the asparagus and cheeses.

3 Beat together the eggs and milk. Add 1/2 tsp salt and pepper to taste. Combine with the asparagus and cheese mixture, and the thyme leaves.

4 Divide the filling evenly among the shells and top with the asparagus tips.

VARIATION

SPINACH: Substitute *1.25 kg (21/2 lb) fresh spinach* for the asparagus, and *1 chopped onion* and *2 finely chopped garlic cloves* for the spring onions. Blanch the spinach in boiling salted water. Drain and refresh; squeeze dry, and cut into strips. Cook the onion and garlic in the oil or butter for about 5 minutes, stirring, until tender. Combine the spinach, onion, and garlic with the cheeses. Add *1 tbsp chopped fresh rosemary and thyme*, and add the spinach mixture to the egg and milk mixture with 1/2 tsp salt and pepper to taste.

HERB & SPRING ONION

*For 8–10 x 10-cm (4-in) quiches
or 1 x 25-cm (10-in) quiche*

INGREDIENTS

*125 g (4 oz) spring onions,
both white and green parts, chopped
1 tbsp olive oil
2 large garlic cloves, finely chopped or crushed
4 eggs, beaten
175 ml (6 fl oz) milk
salt and freshly ground pepper
90 g (3 oz) Gruyère cheese, grated
30 g (1 oz) Parmesan cheese, grated
60 g (2 oz) mixed fresh herbs, such as parsley, tarragon,
dill, thyme, marjoram, chives, and basil (use at least 2 and
not more than 4 types), chopped*

PREPARATION

1 Cook the spring onions in the oil for 3–5 minutes, stirring, until tender. Add the garlic and cook for 1–2 minutes, stirring, until the garlic begins to colour and smell fragrant.

2 Beat together the eggs and milk. Add 1/2 tsp salt and pepper to taste. Stir in the spring onions and garlic, the cheeses, and chopped herbs. Mix together well.

VARIATION

COURGETTE & RED PEPPER: Substitute *750 g (11/2 lb) courgettes, diced*, and *1 large red pepper, cored, seeded, and diced*, for the spring onions. Substitute *3 tbsp chopped fresh parsley* and *1 tsp fresh thyme leaves* or *1/2 tsp dried thyme* for the mixed herbs. Cook the diced pepper in the oil for about 3 minutes until it begins to soften. Add the courgettes, half of the garlic, and salt to taste. Cook over medium-low heat, stirring often, for 10 minutes, or until the courgettes are tender but still bright green. If the vegetables begin to stick to the pan, add *1 tbsp water*. Add the remaining garlic, the herbs, and pepper to taste. Stir for about 1 minute, combine with the cheeses, and add to the egg and milk mixture.

LEEK & GOAT'S CHEESE

For 8–10 x 7-cm (3-in) quiches
or 1 x 25-cm (10-in) quiche

INGREDIENTS

1.25 kg (2¹/2 lb) leeks, trimmed, white parts split in half
lengthways, washed thoroughly, and thinly sliced
2 tbsp butter or olive oil
1 tsp fresh thyme leaves, or ¹/2 tsp dried thyme
salt and freshly ground pepper
3 eggs, beaten
175 ml (6 fl oz) milk
175 g (6 oz) goat's cheese, crumbled
30 g (1 oz) Parmesan cheese, grated

PREPARATION

1 Cook the leeks in the butter or oil, stirring
often, for about 10 minutes, until thoroughly
tender but not browned. Add the thyme, and
salt and pepper to taste, and remove from
the heat.
2 Beat together the eggs, milk, and cheeses. Stir
in a little more salt and pepper. Combine this
mixture with the leeks.

SMOKED SALMON & SPRING ONION

For 8–10 x 7-cm (3-in) quiches
or 1 x 25-cm (10-in) quiche

INGREDIENTS

1 small bunch of spring onions, both white
and green parts, chopped
1 tbsp olive oil
4 eggs, beaten
175 ml (6 fl oz) milk
125 g (4 oz) smoked salmon, diced
salt and freshly ground pepper

PREPARATION

1 Cook the spring onions in the oil for about
5 minutes, stirring, until tender.
2 Beat together the eggs and milk. Add the
smoked salmon and spring onions, and salt and
pepper to taste. Stir well to mix.

VARIATION

PRAWN & CHIVE: Substitute *3 tbsp snipped chives*
for the spring onions and *200 g (7 oz) peeled, cooked*
prawns (defrosted and drained if frozen) for the
smoked salmon.

CHERRY TOMATO & BASIL

For 8–10 x 7-cm (3-in) quiches

INGREDIENTS

4 eggs, beaten
175 ml (6 fl oz) milk
salt and freshly ground pepper
8–10 cherry tomatoes
1 small bunch of fresh basil, slivered

PREPARATION

1 Beat together the eggs and milk, with salt and
pepper to taste.
2 Put a tomato in the centre of each small quiche
shell and slowly pour in the egg and milk
mixture. Sprinkle with the basil.

WILD MUSHROOM & CHEESE

For 8–10 x 7-cm (3-in) quiches
or 1 x 25-cm (10-in) quiche

INGREDIENTS

2 medium shallots, finely chopped
1 tbsp olive oil
500 g (1 lb) fresh wild mushrooms,
cut into 5-mm (¹/4-in) thick slices
salt and freshly ground pepper
3 large garlic cloves, finely chopped or crushed
30 g (1 oz) dried cep mushrooms, soaked and drained (see
page 156), and coarsely chopped
4 tbsp dry white or red wine
1 tbsp soy sauce
1 tbsp chopped fresh sage
1 tsp fresh thyme leaves, or ¹/2 tsp dried thyme
60 g (2 oz) Gruyère cheese, grated
30 g (1 oz) Parmesan cheese, grated
4 eggs, beaten
175 ml (6 fl oz) milk

PREPARATION

1 Cook the shallots in the oil until tender. Add the
fresh mushrooms and a little salt. Cook, stirring,
until the mushrooms begin to release water, then
add the garlic and ceps. Cook for 2 minutes.
2 Add the wine, soy sauce, herbs, and pepper to
taste. Cook, stirring often, until all of the liquid
has evaporated. Divide the mushrooms evenly
among the quiche shells.
3 Combine the cheeses and sprinkle over the
mushroom mixture. Beat together the eggs and
milk, with salt and pepper to taste. Pour over
the mushroom mixture.

CELEBRATING ITALY

*Capture the essence of Italy in a sun-splashed array of dishes that
reflect the national colours of red, white, and green.
The delicious aromatic combination of
tomatoes, garlic, herbs, and olive oil forms
the basis of most Italian finger food.*

Asparagus Frittata
(page 39)

*Beef
Carpaccio
(page 106)*

*Clams on the Half Shell (page 102)
with Tomato Concassée (page 72)
and Basil Pesto (page 25)*

*Pizzettas with Herb & Garlic with Parmesan topping
and Mozzarella & Tomato topping (page 64)*

Coffee Macaroons (page 131)

Almond Biscotti (page 126)

Sun-dried Tomato
Pizzetta

Cherry Tomato
& Chive
Pizzetta

PIZZAS & PIZZETTAS

Versatile is the best word to describe pizzas and pizzettas. I have provided a tempting selection of toppings, which can be made a day ahead and refrigerated. For fast ideas, go to Quick Toppings (see page 70). Pizza dough can be refrigerated for a day or two, or frozen for several months. The dough can be made into large pizzas, then cut into diamond-shaped pieces after baking, or shaped into round, bite-sized pizzettas before baking.

Anchovy & Caper Pizzetta

Mozzarella & Tomato Pizzetta

Olive & Parmesan Pizzetta

TO MAKE PIZZAS & PIZZETTAS

*Makes 2 x 30–35-cm (12–14-in) pizzas
or 16–20 pizzettas*

1 Prepare the dough as directed on page 144.

2 If the dough has not been rolled out before refrigerating or freezing, let it come to room temperature before rolling out your pizza or pizzetta bases. If you have already rolled out the dough, do not defrost it.

3 Prepare your choice of topping from the recipes given on pages 64–65.

4 Add your chosen topping to the pizza or pizzetta bases. In a preheated 230°C (450°F, Gas 8) oven, bake pizzas for 20–25 minutes, and pizzettas for 15–20 minutes, until the crusts are crisp, browned, and fragrant. Serve hot or warm.

A PIZZA PLATTER
A Sweet Pepper pizza cut into diamond-shaped pieces is encircled by pizzettas topped with (clockwise from top) Sun-dried Tomato; Cherry Tomato & Chive; Anchovy & Caper; Mozzarella & Tomato; and Olive & Parmesan.

PIZZA & PIZZETTA TOPPINGS

*Ingredients such as sweet red and yellow peppers cooked slowly in olive oil, luscious wild mushrooms,
ripe tomatoes, and fragrant herbs make mouthwatering toppings for pizzas.*

★

TOMATO & PESTO

For 2 x 30–35-cm (12–14-in) pizzas or 16–20 pizzettas

INGREDIENTS

3–4 large garlic cloves, finely chopped or crushed
1 tbsp olive oil
1·5 kg (3 lb) canned or fresh tomatoes,
peeled, seeded, and chopped
1/4 tsp sugar
salt (preferably sea salt) and freshly ground pepper
1 tsp dried oregano or thyme, or 2 tbsp slivered fresh basil
1 quantity Basil Pesto (see page 25)
60 g (2 oz) Parmesan cheese, grated

PREPARATION

1 Cook the garlic in the oil. When the garlic
begins to colour, add the tomatoes, sugar, salt to
taste, and the dried herbs, if using. Cook, stirring
often, for 20–30 minutes, until the tomatoes are
reduced and the sauce is thickened.
2 Stir in the basil, if using, and cook over gentle
heat for 1–2 minutes. Add pepper to taste and
remove from the heat.
3 Transfer to a food processor fitted with the metal
blade, and work for about 30 seconds. Taste, and
adjust seasonings.
4 Spoon the tomato sauce over the pizza or
pizzetta bases. Add 1 tsp pesto to each pizzetta
base or divide the pesto between the large pizzas.
Sprinkle with the grated Parmesan cheese.

VARIATIONS

SUN-DRIED TOMATO: Substitute *sliced sun-dried
tomatoes* for the pesto, and *1/2 tsp dried oregano* for
the Parmesan cheese.
CHERRY TOMATO & CHIVE: Substitute *sliced cherry
tomatoes* for the pesto, and top the Parmesan
cheese with *fresh chives.*
MOZZARELLA & TOMATO: Substitute *cubes of
mozzarella cheese* for the pesto and Parmesan
cheese, and sprinkle with *chopped fresh herbs.*
OLIVE & PARMESAN: Substitute *sliced stoned black
olives* for the pesto; sprinkle the Parmesan cheese
in the centre.
ANCHOVY & CAPER: Substitute *16 anchovy fillets* for
the pesto, and *4 tbsp capers* for the Parmesan cheese.

TOMATO & CAPER

For 2 x 30–35-cm (12–14-in) pizzas or 16–20 pizzettas

INGREDIENTS

3 tbsp olive oil
60 g (2 oz) Parmesan cheese, grated
8 large garlic cloves, 6 thinly sliced
and 2 finely chopped or crushed
1 kg (2 lb) plum tomatoes, peeled,
juice and seeds squeezed out, and chopped
2 tsp dried oregano, or 2 tbsp chopped fresh basil
salt and freshly ground pepper
4 tbsp capers, drained and rinsed
black olives (optional)
4 artichoke hearts, drained and sliced (optional)
12 anchovy fillets, rinsed and cut in half (optional)

PREPARATION

1 Brush the pizza or pizzetta bases with half of the
olive oil and sprinkle with half of the Parmesan
cheese. Scatter the sliced garlic over the Parmesan.
2 Toss together the tomatoes, the remaining garlic,
the oregano or basil, and salt and pepper to taste.
Spoon over the sliced garlic.
3 Top with the capers, any of the optional
ingredients, and the remaining Parmesan cheese.
Drizzle over the remaining olive oil.

HERB & GARLIC WITH
PARMESAN

For 2 x 30–35-cm (12–14-in) pizzas or 16–20 pizzettas

INGREDIENTS

3 tbsp olive oil
3–4 garlic cloves, finely chopped or crushed
4 tbsp chopped fresh rosemary, sage, or oregano,
or a mixture
30 g (1 oz) Parmesan cheese, grated

PREPARATION

1 Mix together the oil and garlic. Brush each pizza
or pizzetta base generously with this mixture.
2 Sprinkle the chopped herbs over the oil and garlic
mixture. Top with the grated Parmesan cheese.

SWEET PEPPER

For 2 x 30–35-cm (12–14-in) pizzas or 16–20 pizzettas

INGREDIENTS

2 medium onions (optional)
6 large peppers (red and/or yellow), cored, seeded, and cut into long thin strips
3 tbsp olive oil
coarse sea salt and freshly ground pepper
3 large garlic cloves, finely chopped or crushed
2 tbsp slivered fresh basil
2 tsp fresh thyme leaves
500 g (1 lb) tomatoes, peeled, seeded, and chopped

PREPARATION

1 If using the onions, without peeling them, bake them for 1¼ hours in a preheated 200°C (400°F, Gas 6) oven, turning them every 15 minutes.
2 Peel off and discard the burnt outer layers of the onions. Cut the onions into long thin slices.
3 Cook the pepper strips in 1 tbsp of the oil, stirring, until they begin to sizzle, and sprinkle with salt and pepper. Reduce the heat, cover, and cook for 15 minutes, stirring often, until tender.
4 Stir in two-thirds of the garlic, the basil, and thyme, and remove from the heat. Taste, and adjust seasonings.
5 Toss the chopped tomatoes with the remaining garlic and salt and pepper to taste. Layer the tomatoes, peppers, and onions over the pizza or pizzetta bases. Drizzle over the remaining oil.

PROVENÇAL ONION

For 2 x 30–35-cm (12–14-in) pizzas or 16–20 pizzettas

INGREDIENTS

2 kg (4 lb) white or yellow onions, finely chopped
coarse sea salt and freshly ground pepper
5–6 tbsp olive oil
4 garlic cloves, finely chopped or crushed
3–4 tsp fresh thyme leaves, or 1–2 tsp dried thyme
2 tbsp capers, drained, rinsed, and crushed
32 anchovy fillets, rinsed and cut in half
16–20 Niçoise olives

PREPARATION

1 Cook the onions, with about ½ tsp sea salt, in 4 tbsp of the oil. When the onions begin to sizzle, add the garlic, thyme, and pepper to taste.
2 Reduce the heat, cover, and cook for 45 minutes, stirring often. Add the capers, then taste, and adjust seasonings.
3 Spread the mixture over the pizza or pizzetta bases. Top with the anchovies and olives. Drizzle over the remaining oil.

WILD MUSHROOM & HERB

For 2 x 30–35-cm (12–14-in) pizzas or 16–20 pizzettas

INGREDIENTS

2 medium shallots, finely chopped
3 tbsp olive oil
500 g (1 lb) fresh wild mushrooms, trimmed, rinsed, and cut into 5-mm (¼-in) slices
salt and freshly ground pepper
3 large garlic cloves, finely chopped or crushed
30 g (1 oz) dried ceps, soaked and drained (see page 156), and coarsely chopped
4 tbsp dry white or red wine
1 tbsp soy sauce
1 tbsp chopped fresh sage, or 2 tsp chopped fresh rosemary
1 tsp fresh thyme leaves, or ½ tsp dried thyme

PREPARATION

1 Cook the shallots in 1 tbsp of the oil, stirring, until tender and beginning to brown. Add the fresh mushrooms and a little salt. Cook, stirring, until the mushrooms begin to release water.
2 Add the garlic and ceps, and cook for 2 minutes, stirring. Add the wine, soy sauce, herbs, and pepper to taste. Cook until the liquid has just about evaporated from the pan.
3 Spread the mixture over the pizza or pizzetta bases. Drizzle over the remaining oil.

CALZONE & FOCACCIA

Calzone and focaccia are variations of pizzas. Calzone are oval pizzas folded over their toppings to make turnovers. Focaccia is a flat bread like a thick pizza. For parties, I make bite-sized calzone, and cut focaccia into small squares.

★

GOAT'S CHEESE & HERB CALZONE

Makes 36

INGREDIENTS

1 quantity risen pizza dough (see page 144)
500 g (1 lb) mild fresh goat's cheese
3 tbsp plain low-fat yogurt
60 g (2 oz) Parmesan cheese, grated
2 garlic cloves, finely chopped or crushed
125 g (4 oz) fresh herbs, such as parsley, basil, thyme, rosemary, sage, and oregano, chopped
2 tbsp chopped fresh chives
salt and freshly ground pepper
4 tbsp olive oil, mixed with
2 garlic cloves, finely chopped or crushed (optional)

PREPARATION

1 Make pizza dough as directed on page 144, up to the end of step 4. Punch down the dough and divide it into 3 equal pieces. Divide each of these into 6 pieces, then cut each of the 6 pieces in half, to form 36 pieces in all. Form small balls with the pieces, and cover. Let rest for 15 minutes.

2 Mix together the goat's cheese and yogurt. Stir in the Parmesan cheese, garlic, mixed herbs, and chives. Add salt and pepper to taste.

3 Roll out each ball of dough into an oval shape, about 3–5 mm (1/8–1/4 in) thick. Brush with garlic-flavoured oil, if using.

4 Place 2 tsp of the filling on one half of each calzone oval. Fold the top half of the calzone over to meet the bottom edge, making a half-moon shape. Pinch the edges together, then fold the edge in once, and twist it to make an attractive lip.

5 Make one or two small slits in the top of each calzone to allow the steam to escape during baking and prevent the calzone from bursting.

6 Bake the calzone on lightly oiled, cornmeal- or semolina-dusted baking trays, in a preheated 230°C (450°F, Gas 8) oven, for 15–20 minutes, or until the calzone are brown and crisp around the edges.

TOMATO & BASIL CALZONE

Makes 36

INGREDIENTS

1 quantity risen pizza dough (see page 144)
2 garlic cloves, finely chopped or crushed
1 tbsp olive oil
1.5 kg (3 lb) canned or fresh tomatoes, peeled, seeded, and chopped
1/4 tsp sugar
salt and freshly ground pepper
3 tbsp slivered fresh basil
90 g (3 oz) mozzarella cheese, cut into 36 pieces
Parmesan cheese, grated

PREPARATION

1 Make pizza dough as directed on page 144, up to the end of step 4. Punch down the dough and divide it into 3 equal pieces. Divide each of these into 6 pieces, then cut each of the 6 pieces in half, to form 36 pieces in all. Form small balls with the pieces, and cover. Let rest for 15 minutes.

2 Cook the garlic in the olive oil. Add the tomatoes with the sugar, and salt to taste. Cook, stirring often, until the tomatoes are reduced. Remove from the heat.

3 Stir in the basil with pepper to taste.

4 Roll out each ball of dough into an oval shape, about 3–5 mm (1/8–1/4 in) thick.

5 Place 1 heaped tsp tomato sauce on one half of each calzone oval, top with a piece of mozzarella and a pinch of grated Parmesan cheese. Fold the top half of the calzone over to meet the bottom edge, making a half-moon shape. Pinch the edges together, then fold the edge in once, and twist it to make an attractive lip.

6 Make one or two small slits in the top of each calzone to allow the steam to escape during baking and prevent the calzone from bursting.

7 Bake the calzone on lightly oiled, cornmeal- or semolina-dusted baking trays, in a preheated 230°C (450°F, Gas 8) oven, for 15–20 minutes, or until the calzone are brown and crisp around the edges.

MUSHROOM & RICOTTA CALZONE

Makes 36

INGREDIENTS

1 quantity risen pizza dough (see page 144)
1 garlic clove, finely chopped or crushed
1 tbsp olive oil
60 g (2 oz) dried ceps, soaked and drained (see page 156)
and coarsely chopped
2 tbsp dry white wine
2 tsp chopped fresh rosemary
1 tsp fresh thyme leaves
salt and freshly ground pepper
375 g (12 oz) low-fat ricotta cheese
90 g (3 oz) Parmesan cheese, grated

PREPARATION

1 Make pizza dough as directed on page 144, up to the end of step 4. Punch down the dough and divide it into 3 equal pieces. Divide each of these into 6 pieces, then cut each of the 6 pieces in half, to form 36 pieces. Form small balls with the pieces, and cover. Let rest for 15 minutes.
2 Cook the garlic in the oil until it begins to colour. Add the ceps and stir for 1 minute. Add the wine, herbs, and salt and pepper to taste.
3 Mix the two cheeses into the mushroom mixture.
4 Roll out each ball of dough into an oval shape, about 3–5 mm (1/8–1/4 in) thick.
5 Place 2 tsp of the filling on one half of each calzone oval. Fold the top half of the calzone over to meet the bottom edge, making a half-moon shape. Pinch the edges together, then fold the edge in once, and twist it to make an attractive lip.
6 Make one or two small slits in the top of each calzone to allow the steam to escape during baking and prevent the calzone from bursting.
7 Bake the calzone on lightly oiled, cornmeal- or semolina-dusted baking trays, in a preheated 230°C (450°F, Gas 8) oven, for 15–20 minutes, or until the calzone are brown and crisp around the edges.

ITALIAN FAST FOOD

Focaccia is the traditional pizza base. In Italy it is also served as a savoury bread, often garnished with herbs, or it is slit, filled with ham, cheese, or salami, and cut into pieces to form sandwiches.

SAGE & ONION FOCACCIA

Makes 35 x 5-cm (2-in) squares

INGREDIENTS

1 quantity focaccia dough (see page 145)
5 tbsp olive oil
750 g (1 1/2 lb) onions, chopped
1/2 tsp coarse sea salt
30 fresh sage leaves, chopped, more for garnish

PREPARATION

1 Make focaccia dough as directed on page 145, up to the end of step 5, but do not shape into balls.
2 Heat 2 tbsp of the oil in a heavy-based non-stick frying pan over medium heat. Add the onions and salt. Cook, stirring, for 15 minutes, until the onions are tender and beginning to brown.
3 Remove the onions from the heat and stir in the chopped sage. Let cool.
4 Meanwhile, shape the dough into 2 balls as directed in step 5 on page 145 and continue until the end of step 6. Brush the focaccia with olive oil and spread the onion and sage mixture over the tops. Cover, and let rise for 1 hour.
5 Bake in a preheated 200°C (400°F, Gas 6) oven, preferably with a baking stone (see page 156), for 20–25 minutes.
6 Cool on racks, then cut into 5-cm (2-in) squares and garnish with small sage leaves.

OLIVE FOCACCIA

Makes 35 x 5-cm (2-in) squares

INGREDIENTS

1 quantity focaccia dough (see page 145)
250 g (8 oz) black olives, stoned and chopped,
more for garnish (optional)
1 tbsp olive oil

PREPARATION

1 Make focaccia dough as directed on page 145 up to the end of step 3, but do not shape into balls.
2 Add the olives to the focaccia dough, and knead again to incorporate them evenly.
3 Shape the dough into a ball, and proceed from step 4 in the basic recipe on page 145. If you prefer, garnish the focaccia with black olives set in the dimples before baking.
4 Cut into 5-cm (2-in) squares.

RUSTIC ITALIAN BRUSCHETTA & CROSTINI

Thank goodness the boring canapés of yesteryear have given way to today's gutsy, Mediterranean-inspired bruschetta and crostini. Bruschetta are crisp on the outside but still bready in the centre, while crostini are smaller and more crisp, rather like croûtons. Bruschetta and crostini can only be as good as the bread they are made from. I like to make my own sourdough or herbed bread, but for a large party, I buy the best hard-crusted country bread or herb bread available for bruschetta, and baguettes to make crostini.

CROSTINI
Croûton-like crostini make crisp bases for any number of Italian-style toppings, including Tomato & Mozzarella.

Tomato & Mozzarella Crostini

Anchovy Bruschetta

BRUSCHETTA
Unpretentious canapés, bruschetta conceal a soft interior within thick, crusty slices. Piquant toppings, such as Anchovy, garnished with capers and spring onions, and Roast Pepper & Mozzarella, with sliced pepperoni and flaked tuna, add to their rustic appeal.

Roast Pepper & Mozzarella Bruschetta

TO MAKE BRUSCHETTA & CROSTINI

Makes 18–24 bruschetta and 9–12 crostini

1 FOR BRUSCHETTA, cut 1 loaf of crusty bread into 9–12 x 2-cm (¾-in) thick slices.

2 Set under a preheated grill, about 10–12 cm (4–5 in) from the heat, and toast for 1 minute, or less, per side – the bread should remain soft inside.

3 Remove the toasted slices of bread from the heat and immediately rub them vigorously with 1–2 large garlic cloves, sliced in half lengthways. Brush with 2–3 tbsp olive oil. Cut the slices in half. Keep the bruschetta warm in a low oven.

4 Top with your chosen topping and heat through (see recipes on pages 70–71).

1 FOR CROSTINI, cut 1 large baguette into 9–12 x 1-cm (½-in) thick slices.

2 Set under a preheated grill, about 10–12 cm (4–5 in) from the heat, and toast until lightly browned on both sides.

3 If serving the same day, rub the bread with 1–2 large garlic cloves, sliced in half lengthways, then brush with 2–3 tbsp olive oil. If making in advance, let cool, then keep in an airtight container for up to 2 days. Rub with garlic and brush with olive oil before topping and serving.

4 Top with your chosen topping and heat through (see recipes on pages 70–71).

Tomato & Mozzarella Crostini

Anchovy Bruschetta

Roast Pepper & Mozzarella Bruschetta

BRUSCHETTA & CROSTINI TOPPINGS

Add any of these luscious toppings to garlic-scented, toasted bread to create gastronomic appetizers. Robust flavours from typical Mediterranean ingredients, such as peppers and tomatoes, anchovies, and capers, add to the pleasure of biting into the crunchy bases.

★

ROAST PEPPER & MOZZARELLA

For 18–24 bruschetta or 36–48 crostini

INGREDIENTS

1 kg (2 lb) red peppers, or a combination of red and yellow peppers
2 large garlic cloves, finely chopped or crushed
2 tbsp olive oil
2 tbsp slivered fresh basil leaves
coarse sea salt and freshly ground pepper
125 g (4 oz) fresh or smoked mozzarella cheese, cut into thin slivers

PREPARATION

1 Bake the peppers in a preheated 200°C (400°F, Gas 6) oven for 30–45 minutes, turning every 10 minutes, until the peppers are soft and the skin is puffed and brown in places.

2 Transfer to a bowl, cover with a well-fitting plate, and let cool for 20–30 minutes, by which time the peppers will have softened and released plenty of liquid. Reduce the oven temperature to 190°C (375°F, Gas 5).

3 Peel, core, and halve the peppers over a bowl to catch the juices. Remove the seeds and white ribs. Slice the peppers into thin strips, and place in another bowl.

4 Strain the reserved juices over the peppers. Toss with the garlic, olive oil, basil, and salt and pepper to taste. Marinate for at least 30 minutes.

5 Place a sliver of mozzarella on each bruschetta or crostini, and top with the pepper mixture. Bake in the oven for 5–10 minutes, until the cheese begins to melt. Serve hot.

🕐 *The roasted peppers in their marinade, but without the garlic and basil, will keep up to a week in the refrigerator. Add the garlic and basil only a few hours before serving.*

Quick Toppings

There are many ingredients, such as ready-made bottled sauces and dips, that can be used to make delicious toppings for bruschetta and crostini in a matter of minutes. Here are just a few of my suggestions:

PESTO: *Pesto with cooked scallops and cooked peeled prawns, garnished with fresh basil or chervil.*

SALSA: *Salsa with cooked scallops, cooked peeled prawns, chopped smoked turkey, or smoked trout, garnished with fresh coriander.*

FROMAGE BLANC: *Fromage blanc, crème fraîche, or ricotta cheese, with caviar spooned in the centre.*

HUMMUS: *Hummus sprinkled with fresh parsley or garnished with thin lemon slices.*

TARAMASALATA: *Taramasalata garnished with salmon roe.*

RICOTTA: *Ricotta cheese with slivered sun-dried tomatoes or sliced Italian or French dried sausage.*

PATE: *Any meat, fish, or vegetable pâté sprinkled with chopped fresh herbs.*

CANNED WHITE BEAN: *Canned white beans or chick peas, mashed and seasoned with lemon juice, olive oil, and garlic, sprinkled with chopped fresh herbs or topped with sliced dried sausage or smoked ham.*

FRESH HERB: *Fresh herbs, such as tarragon, basil, dill, chervil, and parsley, washed and chopped with scissors.*

SMOKED MACKEREL: *Canned smoked mackerel, drained and flaked, topped with thin slices of lemon.*

SMOKED SALMON: *Thin slices of smoked salmon topped with capers.*

TOMATO & OLIVE: *Bottled tomato sauce garnished with stoned black olives.*

ROCKET & PARMESAN: *Chopped rocket leaves garnished with thin slivers of Parmesan cheese.*

ANCHOVY

For 18–24 bruschetta or 36–48 crostini

INGREDIENTS

1–2 garlic cloves, peeled
24 oil-packed anchovy fillets, rinsed, or 12 salt-packed
anchovies, well rinsed and boned
3 tbsp olive oil
2 tbsp red wine vinegar
freshly ground pepper

PREPARATION

1 Pound garlic to taste in a pestle and mortar. Add
the anchovy fillets and continue pounding. Add
the olive oil, wine vinegar, and pepper to taste,
and pound to a coarse paste.
2 Spread a thin, even layer of anchovy paste over
bruschetta or crostini and serve, or heat through
in a preheated 180°C (350°F, Gas 4) oven for
10–15 minutes before serving.

 *This topping can be made in advance and kept in
the refrigerator for 2 days. If making in advance,
you may want to use less garlic, because the garlic
will taste stronger after a day or two.*

TOMATO & CAPER

For 18–24 bruschetta or 36–48 crostini

INGREDIENTS

1 small onion, chopped
1 tbsp olive oil
8 large garlic cloves, finely chopped or crushed
1 kg (2 lb) ripe tomatoes, peeled, seeded, and chopped
90 g (3 oz) capers, rinsed and chopped in a food processor
salt and freshly ground pepper

PREPARATION

1 Cook the onion in the oil, stirring, for about
5 minutes, until tender. Add the garlic to the
pan. Cook, stirring, for about 1 minute, until
the garlic begins to colour.
2 Add the tomatoes, capers, a small amount of
salt, and pepper to taste. Cook over medium
heat for 15–20 minutes, stirring often, or until
the tomatoes have reduced.
3 Remove the sauce from the heat, and taste and
adjust seasonings. Spread over bruschetta or
crostini and serve hot.

 *This topping can be made in advance and kept in
the refrigerator for 2–3 days.*

TOMATO & MOZZARELLA

For 18–24 bruschetta or 36–48 crostini

INGREDIENTS

3–4 large garlic cloves, finely chopped or crushed
1 tbsp olive oil
1 kg (2 lb) tomatoes, peeled, seeded, and chopped
pinch of sugar
salt, preferably sea salt, and freshly ground pepper
1/2 tsp dried thyme (optional)
2 tbsp slivered fresh basil
125 g (4 oz) fresh mozzarella cheese, cut into thin slivers

PREPARATION

1 Cook the garlic in the oil until it begins to colour,
then add the tomatoes, sugar, salt, and dried thyme,
if using. Cook, stirring often, for 15–20 minutes,
or until the tomatoes have reduced.
2 Stir in the basil and cook for 1 minute. Add
pepper to taste and remove the mixture from the
heat. Taste, and adjust the seasonings.
3 Place a sliver of mozzarella on each bruschetta or
crostini, and top with the tomato sauce. Place on
a baking tray and bake in a preheated 190°C
(375°F, Gas 5) oven for 5–10 minutes, until the
cheese begins to melt. Serve hot.

*This topping can be made in advance and kept in
the refrigerator for 3–4 days.*

RUSTIC CANAPES

*Like much of Italian food, bruschetta and crostini derive
from an unpretentious rural tradition.*

*Thick, flat slices of Italian country bread, bruschetta
originated in antiquity — there are records of them from
Roman times. Traditionally, they are grilled over charcoal,
then rubbed with garlic, doused with extra-virgin olive oil,
and liberally sprinkled with salt and pepper.*

*The word bruschetta actually derives from the Italian
bruscare, to roast over coals. Bruschetta are always served
warm in Italy, either as a snack at any time of day or as an
appetizer before the main meal.*

*Crostini, the Italian for croûtons, are more delicate than
bruschetta and are often fashioned into fancy shapes and
buttered before being toasted or baked. Bite-sized crostini
are also added to soup.*

*Crostini are particularly popular in the Italian region
of Tuscany, where meaty toppings, especially game, are the
preferred choice. Crostini with chicken liver topping is one
of the region's best-known specialities.*

CAPONATA

*This sweet-and-sour vegetable stew from Sicily makes a
great topping for bruschetta and crostini. It keeps for
1 week in the refrigerator.
For 18–24 bruschetta or 36–48 crostini*

INGREDIENTS

*4 ripe fresh tomatoes, or 8 canned Italian plum tomatoes,
peeled, seeded, and finely chopped
salt and freshly ground pepper
2 medium aubergines, peeled and cut into 1-cm
(1/2-in) dice, sprinkled with salt, and drained for 1 hour
2 large red peppers, cored, seeded, and diced
2 medium courgettes, diced
2 medium onions, chopped
4 large garlic cloves, finely chopped or crushed
2 heaped tbsp capers, rinsed
2 tbsp raisins
1 bay leaf
1 tsp fresh thyme leaves, or 1/2 tsp dried thyme
4 tbsp white wine vinegar, sherry vinegar,
or cider vinegar
1 tbsp sugar
2 tbsp olive oil*

PREPARATION

1 Combine the tomatoes and a pinch of salt in
a pan. Cook over low heat, stirring, for
15 minutes. Mash, and set aside.

2 Rinse the aubergines, and dry. Transfer them
to an oiled baking dish.

3 Add the tomatoes, the remaining vegetables,
garlic, capers, raisins, bay leaf, thyme, and salt
and pepper to taste. Mix together.

4 Combine the vinegar and the sugar in a
saucepan and heat until the sugar just dissolves.
Pour over the vegetables. Add the olive oil and
toss together.

5 Cover the baking dish tightly and bake in a
preheated 180°C (350°F, Gas 4) oven for
1½–2 hours, stirring every 30 minutes, until
the vegetables are tender and fragrant.

6 Let cool, then taste, and adjust seasonings.
Spread the mixture over bruschetta or crostini
and serve hot.

TOMATO CONCASSEE

For 18–24 bruschetta or 36–48 crostini

INGREDIENTS

*750 g (1 1/2 lb) tomatoes, peeled, seeded, and finely chopped
1 tbsp balsamic vinegar
1 tbsp olive oil
1–2 large garlic cloves, finely chopped or crushed
2–3 tbsp slivered fresh basil
coarse sea salt and freshly ground pepper*

PREPARATION

1 Toss together the tomatoes, vinegar, and oil
with the garlic, basil, salt, and pepper to taste.
Let stand for 15 minutes or longer.

2 Spread the mixture evenly over bruschetta
or crostini and serve.

WILD MUSHROOM

For 18–24 bruschetta or 36–48 crostini

INGREDIENTS

*2 medium shallots, finely chopped
2 tbsp olive oil
500 g (1 lb) fresh wild mushrooms,
stalks trimmed, thoroughly cleaned and dried, sliced
5-mm (1/4-in) thick
salt and freshly ground pepper
4 large garlic cloves, finely chopped or crushed
30 g (1 oz) dried cep mushrooms, soaked and drained
(see page 156), coarsely chopped
4 tbsp dry white or red wine
2 tsp soy sauce
2 tsp chopped fresh rosemary
1 tsp fresh thyme leaves, or 1/2 tsp dried thyme*

PREPARATION

1 Cook the shallots in the oil over medium heat,
stirring, for about 5 minutes, until tender.

2 Add the mushrooms and a little salt and cook,
stirring, until they begin to release water, then
add the garlic and ceps.

3 Cook, stirring, for 2 minutes, then add the
wine, soy sauce, rosemary, thyme, and pepper
to taste. Cook, for about 10 minutes, stirring,
until all of the liquid has evaporated.

4 Add 2 tbsp of the soaking liquid from the dried
mushrooms if the mushrooms begin to stick
to the pan. Remove from the heat. Taste, and
adjust seasonings. Let cool and chop the
mixture very fine. Spread over bruschetta or
crostini and serve hot.

Wraps, Rolls & Crisps

*When it comes to impressing guests with beautiful,
easy-to-eat finger foods, savoury fillings in
various types of wrappers or on crispy chips are ideal.
The recipes in this section come from far-flung corners
of the world. There are flaky filo pastries and
lemony stuffed vine leaves from Greece and the
Middle East; nachos with piquant toppings from
Mexico; sushi, wontons, and soft
and crispy spring rolls from the Far East.*

FILO PASTRIES

Paper-thin filo is Greek strudel pastry, and the multi-layered morsels made with it crumble in the mouth into fragile flakes. You can buy ready-made filo or you can make it yourself (see page 143). I usually make triangles (*tiropites*), but you can also make cigars, or money bags and parcels as shown here. Full instructions for making all of these shapes are given on pages 142–143.

Pepper

Sea salt

TO MAKE FILO PASTRIES

250 g (8 oz) filo pastry makes about 60 pastry shapes

1 Make the filling of your choice (see pages 76–77).

2 Heat 4 tbsp olive oil with 4 tbsp butter over very low heat until the butter melts.

3 Take one sheet of filo pastry at a time, and keep the rest of the pastry wrapped in a damp tea towel so that it does not dry out.

4 Wrap the filo pastry around the filling, following the directions for the different shapes on pages 142–143.

5 Place the pastries on a non-stick or lightly oiled baking tray. Brush the tops of the pastries with the remaining oil and butter and bake in a preheated 180°C (350°F, Gas 4) oven for 30 minutes, until golden brown. Serve warm.

You can make the fillings and assemble the pastries a day in advance, or freeze them, uncooked, weeks in advance. Only bake them just before serving.

To store, place uncooked pastries on an oiled baking tray, cover, and refrigerate.

To freeze, wrap about 12 uncooked pastries in foil, crimp the edges of the foil tightly, seal in plastic bags, and freeze.

Cooking tip: *If you have frozen the pastries, do not defrost, but transfer them directly from the freezer to the oven, brushing them first with a little oil or melted butter. They may require an extra 5–10 minutes baking.*

Feta cheese

Beaten egg

Rosemary

Thyme

Parsley

Garlic

CRISP & CRUMBLY
Spinach & Feta Cheese filling is encased in filo parcels tied with carrot strips and decorated with coriander leaves, and in filo money bags lightly sprinkled with red paprika.

Nutmeg

Filo
pastry

Onion

Oil

Spinach

FILO PASTRY FILLINGS

Filo pastries can be filled with an endless variety and combination of fresh-tasting ingredients, which can include vegetables, meat, fish, herbs, and cheese – especially Greek feta cheese.

★

SPINACH & FETA CHEESE

Spinach and cheese, a favourite Mediterranean combination, is one of the best known of Greek savoury pastry fillings.
For about 60 pastries

INGREDIENTS

1 kg (2 lb) spinach, stalks removed, leaves washed
salt and freshly ground pepper
1 tbsp olive oil
1 medium onion, chopped
3 garlic cloves, finely chopped or crushed
1 bunch flat-leaf parsley, finely chopped
2 tbsp chopped fresh rosemary,
or 2 tsp crumbled dried rosemary
2 tsp fresh thyme, or 1 tsp dried thyme
2 eggs
250 g (8 oz) feta cheese, crumbled
pinch of freshly grated nutmeg

PREPARATION

1 Blanch the spinach in boiling salted water for 1–2 minutes. Alternatively, put the spinach in a dry non-stick frying pan with only the water left on the leaves after washing. Toss over high heat for 1–2 minutes, until wilted.
2 Rinse the spinach under cold water, squeeze dry in a tea towel, and chop roughly.
3 Heat the olive oil over medium heat in a large frying pan and add the onion. Cook, stirring, until tender and just beginning to brown.
4 Add the garlic, stir together for about 30 seconds, then stir in the spinach, parsley, rosemary, and thyme. Remove from the heat.
5 Beat the eggs in a large bowl and add the feta cheese. Add the spinach mixture, and salt and pepper to taste. Stir in the nutmeg and mix everything together well.

FISH & CORIANDER

This filling does not keep or freeze well, so make it on the day you bake the pastries.
For about 60 pastries

INGREDIENTS

1.25 kg (2½ lb) cod, whiting,
or snapper fillets
60 g (2 oz) fresh coriander, chopped
4 tbsp chopped fresh mint
2 tbsp chopped fresh chives
1 large red pepper, cored, seeded,
and finely chopped
2–3 garlic cloves, finely chopped or crushed
juice of 2 large lemons
2 tbsp olive oil
2 eggs, beaten
½ tsp ground cumin
salt and freshly ground pepper

PREPARATION

1 Steam the fish for about 7 minutes, until just tender. The fish should separate into segments when pierced with a fork. Transfer to a colander and let drain for 5 minutes.
2 Transfer the fish to a large bowl and flake the fillets with your fingers or with a fork. Remove all bones (there are always some in cod fillets).
3 Once you have made sure that all bones have been removed, transfer the flaked fish to a food processor. Process for a few seconds until the fish is finely chopped.
4 Return to the bowl and toss with the remaining ingredients, adding salt and pepper to taste.

FETA CHEESE

Feta cheese is a classic Greek cheese, traditionally made from ewe's milk, although it is now usually made from cow's milk. Because it is preserved in brine, it is sometimes referred to as "pickled cheese". Feta cheese is widely used in Greek and Mediterranean cooking.

LAMB & GREEN VEGETABLE

There is a Middle-Eastern influence in this warmly spiced
filling of minced lamb with sautéed green vegetables.
For about 60 pastries

INGREDIENTS

250 g (8 oz) minced lamb
1 tsp ground allspice
1 tsp ground nutmeg
1 tsp ground cinnamon
salt and freshly ground pepper
90 ml (3 fl oz) water
juice of 1 lemon
1 tbsp olive oil
2 celery stalks, finely chopped
6 spring onions, both white and green parts, finely chopped
2 leeks, trimmed, cleaned, and finely chopped
175 g (6 oz) frozen chopped spinach, defrosted and drained
4 tbsp finely chopped fresh parsley

PREPARATION

1 In a large non-stick saucepan, cook the minced
lamb for 5 minutes – it will fry in its own fat.
Add all of the spices, salt to taste, and 1 tsp
pepper. Cook, stirring, for another 5 minutes.

2 Add the water and lemon juice, and bring to a
boil. Simmer for 15 minutes.

3 Meanwhile, in another saucepan, heat the oil,
and sauté the celery, spring onions, and leeks for
5–7 minutes, until softened.

4 Stir in the spinach and heat through. Add the
vegetables to the lamb, and then add the parsley.
Cook for another 10 minutes. Taste, and
adjust seasonings.

Quick & Easy Fillings

If you are short of time, try these simple ideas. They give a
delicious – and unusual – Oriental flavour to the pastries.

PRAWN & CORIANDER: Sauté *250 g (8 oz) peeled,*
cooked prawns, finely chopped, with *1 garlic clove,*
crushed, in *1 tbsp olive oil* for 5 minutes. Add *2 tbsp*
finely chopped coriander, 1 tsp finely grated lime zest,
and *2 tsp lime juice.*

STIR–FRIED CHICKEN: Sauté *250 g (8 oz) chicken*
breast, skinned and finely chopped, with *4 spring onions,*
thinly sliced, and *2 tsp finely chopped fresh root ginger*
in *1 tbsp peanut oil.* Mix in a bowl with *1 tbsp soy*
sauce, 1 tbsp rice vinegar, 1 tbsp cornflour, and *1 tsp*
sesame oil.

LEEK & FETA CHEESE

The sweet flavour of leeks, which emerges with gentle
cooking, contrasts beautifully with the rich saltiness of
feta cheese in this filling.
For about 60 pastries

INGREDIENTS

1.25 kg (2½ lb) leeks
2 tbsp olive oil
1 tsp fresh thyme leaves, or ½ tsp dried thyme
salt and freshly ground pepper
2 eggs, beaten
175 g (6 oz) feta cheese, crumbled
60 g (2 oz) Parmesan cheese, grated
1 bunch flat-leaf parsley, chopped
30 g (1 oz) fresh dill, chopped

PREPARATION

1 Trim the leeks and discard the green parts that
are tough. Split the white parts lengthways in
half, wash thoroughly, and slice thinly.

2 Heat the oil in a large, heavy-based non-stick
frying pan over medium-low heat and add
the leeks. Cook for about 10 minutes, stirring
often, until the leeks are thoroughly tender but
not browned. Add the thyme, and salt and
pepper to taste. Remove from the heat.

3 Mix together the beaten eggs and feta cheese.
Add the leeks and remaining ingredients and stir
together well.

This filling can be made 1–2 days before
making the pastries.

DOLMADES

Homemade *dolmades*, or stuffed vine leaves, have a marvellous, fresh, lemony flavour. The main ingredients of these leafy parcels are rice and plenty of fresh herbs. Serve them warm or cold.

★

RICE & HERB DOLMADES
Makes about 80

INGREDIENTS

3 tbsp olive oil
1 medium red or white onion, finely chopped
125 g (4 oz) spring onions,
both white and green parts, chopped
250 g (8 oz) long-grain rice
2–3 garlic cloves, finely chopped or crushed
1 tsp ground cumin
salt and freshly ground pepper
500 ml (16 fl oz) water
30 g (1 oz) fresh dill, chopped
30 g (1 oz) fresh parsley, chopped
15 g (1/2 oz) fresh fennel, chopped
4 tbsp chopped fresh mint, or
1 1/2 tsp dried mint
1 egg, beaten
90 vine leaves (fresh or preserved in brine)
juice of 2 large lemons

PREPARATION

1 Heat 2 tbsp of the oil in a large heavy-based frying pan, add the onion and spring onions, and cook over medium heat for about 5 minutes, stirring, until the onions are translucent.
2 Add the rice and cook for 3–5 minutes, stirring, until very lightly browned. Stir in garlic to taste, the cumin, 1/2 tsp salt, and the water. Bring to a boil and simmer for 10 minutes, until the water has been absorbed. The rice will not be cooked through. Remove from the heat and let cool.
3 Stir in the herbs with salt and pepper to taste. Add the egg and combine well.
4 If using preserved vine leaves, rinse them well. Bring a large pan of water to a rolling boil and drop in the vine leaves, several at a time. Blanch preserved vine leaves for about 30 seconds, fresh leaves for 3–5 minutes, until softened. Remove and drain well in a colander or on paper towels.
5 Brush the bottom of a wide, heavy-based saucepan with the remaining oil. Add about 3 tbsp water, and cover with a layer of vine leaves, glossy-side down. Use any torn leaves for this.

6 Snip off the stalks of the remaining vine leaves and make the dolmades by filling and folding them as directed on page 79.
7 Place the dolmades seam-side down in the pan, on top of the layer of leaves, and squeeze them together in tightly packed layers. Pour over the lemon juice, then pour in enough water to cover.
8 Place a small plate on top to keep the dolmades intact while cooking, then cover the pan with a lid. Bring to a boil over medium heat, reduce the heat, and simmer for 2 hours, until the vine leaves are tender.
9 Carefully remove the dolmades from the water with a slotted spoon and allow to drain on racks set over plates, for 15 minutes or longer.

VARIATION

RICE & MEAT DOLMADES: Substitute the following filling for the filling in the main recipe. Cook *1 medium onion, finely chopped*, in *2 tbsp olive oil*, stirring, for about 5 minutes, until translucent. Add *250 g (8 oz) lean minced lamb*, and cook, stirring, until browned. Break up the meat with the back of a wooden spoon so that it does not form lumps. Add *150 g (5 oz) long-grain rice*, *2–3 garlic cloves, finely chopped or crushed*, *1 tsp ground allspice*, and *1 tsp ground cumin*. Cook for about 3 minutes, stirring, until the rice just begins to toast. Turn the heat to low and stir in *350 ml (12 fl oz) water*. Bring to a boil and simmer for 10 minutes, or until the water has been absorbed. The rice will not be cooked through. Remove from heat and let cool. Stir in *4 tbsp chopped fresh mint*, *30 g (1 oz) fresh parsley, chopped*, and *salt and freshly ground pepper to taste*. Add *1 beaten egg*, and combine well. Make the dolmades following steps 4–9 above.

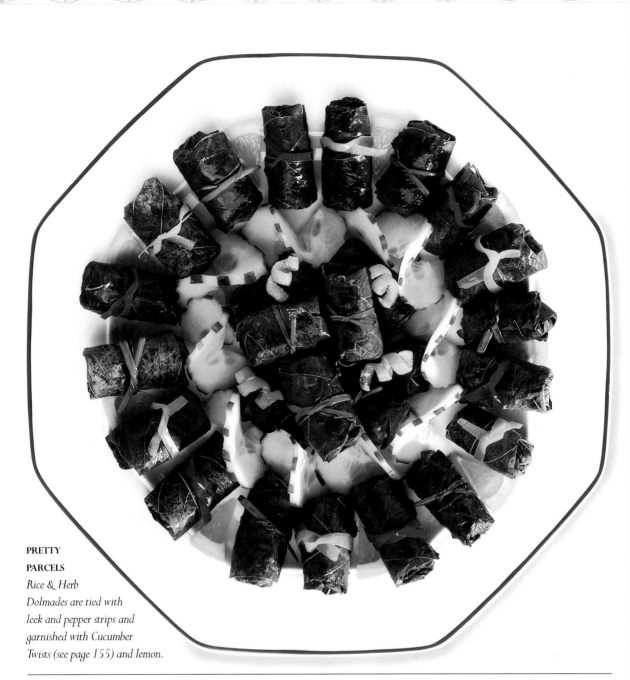

PRETTY PARCELS
Rice & Herb Dolmades are tied with leek and pepper strips and garnished with Cucumber Twists (see page 155) and lemon.

FILLING & FOLDING DOLMADES

1 Lay a blanched leaf, glossy-side down (vein-side up), with the stalk end nearest to you. Place 1 heaped tsp of filling in the middle of the leaf.

2 Fold one side of the leaf over the filling, then fold the other side of the leaf over the filling.

3 Roll up the leaf tightly from the stalk end. Repeat with the remaining leaves and filling. The stuffed leaves should form 2.5-cm (1-in) long parcels.

NACHOS

Add spice to any party by serving nachos – crunchy nacho chips topped with exciting Latin-American flavours. Nacho chips are made from tortillas cut into bite-sized chips or pieces and deep-fried. You can use ready-made nacho chips, which come in different shapes, if you don't want to deep-fry your own tortilla chips, but home-made chips are infinitely better than most commercial chips, which tend to be oversalted and quite oily. Make nacho chips well in advance and store them in airtight tins. You can also serve bowls of home-made nacho chips on their own to accompany drinks and dips. Some nachos are served cold, and others hot, see the recipes on pages 82–83 for full-flavoured meat, fish, and vegetable toppings.

Guacamole & Tomato Nachos

Guacamole & Tomato Nachos

Smoked Salmon Nachos

TO MAKE NACHO CHIPS

Makes 48 chips

1 Cut 12 corn tortillas into quarters. Heat 1 litre (1¾ pints) sunflower or rapeseed oil in a wide saucepan or deep-fat fryer to 180°C (350°F).

2 Deep-fry the tortilla quarters in batches of 4–8. They should float to the top and turn golden brown in seconds. Remove immediately with a skimmer or slotted spoon and drain on paper towels.

3 Allow the oil to reheat to 180°C (350°F) between batches to maintain the correct temperature. When all of the chips are done, salt them lightly.

LIGHT & SPICY
Guacamole & Tomato Nachos and Black Bean Nachos evoke the true taste of Latin America, while Smoked Salmon Nachos and Chicken Nachos provide a contrast with milder flavours.

Black Bean Nachos

Chicken Nachos

Smoked Salmon Nachos

BLACK BEAN NACHOS

*This is a popular Mexican dish, which I make extra thick
when I am using it as a topping for nacho chips.*
Makes 48

INGREDIENTS

2 tbsp sunflower or rapeseed oil
1 large onion, chopped
4 large garlic cloves, finely chopped or crushed
375 g (12 oz) dried black beans, soaked overnight
in 3 litres (5 pints) water
salt
2 litres (3 1/2 pints) water
2 tbsp chopped fresh coriander
2 tsp ground cumin
2 tsp chilli powder
48 nacho chips
125 g (4 oz) Cheddar cheese, grated
6 tbsp crème fraîche or plain low-fat yogurt
Green Tomatillo Salsa (see page 47) or chopped tomatillos
fresh coriander, for garnish

PREPARATION

1 Heat half of the oil in a large, heavy-based
saucepan and sauté the onion with a quarter of
the garlic for about 3 minutes, until the onion
begins to soften.
2 Drain the beans and add to the pan with the 2 litres
(3 1/2 pints) water. Add another quarter of the
garlic, and bring to a boil. Reduce the heat,
cover, and simmer for 1 hour.
3 Add salt to taste, the remaining garlic, and
the coriander, and simmer for about 1 hour, until
the beans are soft and the liquid has thickened
and become aromatic.
4 Let cool, then drain off about two-thirds of
the liquid, and reserve. Mash half of the bean
mixture coarsely in a food processor or with a
potato masher in batches. Stir back into the
remaining bean mixture.
5 Heat the remaining oil in a large non-stick pan
over medium-high heat, and add the cumin, chilli
powder, and a pinch of salt. Cook until the spices
begin to sizzle, then add the beans. (This can be
done in batches if your pan is not large enough to
hold all the beans together.)
6 Fry the beans for 15–20 minutes, mashing with
the back of a wooden spoon and stirring often,
until they begin to get crusty and aromatic. If they
seem too dry, add some of the reserved cooking
liquid. The beans should bubble, thicken, and
reduce, forming a thin crust on the bottom of the
pan, which you should stir back into the mixture.

7 Place the nacho chips on baking trays and
sprinkle with the grated cheese. Place in a
preheated 190°C (375°F, Gas 5) oven for
5–10 minutes, until the cheese melts.
8 Spread the refried beans over the cheese, and
top with crème fraîche or yogurt and salsa or
chopped tomatillos. Garnish with coriander.

Quick Nacho Toppings

*Nacho toppings do not necessarily have to be elaborate. For
a quick snack, you can top the crisp chips with an assortment
of tasty ingredients, most of which are readily available from
supermarkets or delicatessens, or which have been prepared in
advance. Here are some suggestions:*

SMOKED SALMON: *Diced avocado and tomatoes topped with
smoked salmon, and garnished with onion slivers and sprigs
of fresh dill.*
PRAWN & TOMATO: *Fresh Tomato Salsa (see page 29) and
peeled, cooked prawns, garnished with lime and sprigs of
fresh dill.*
CHICKEN: *Shredded cooked chicken tossed with finely diced
celery or spring onion and soured cream, and garnished with
slivers of red pepper.*
CEVICHE: *Ceviche (see page 104), made with very finely
chopped fish and vegetables and drained, garnished with
chopped coriander.*

Prawn & Tomato Nachos

GUACAMOLE NACHOS

My guacamole is mild, with no hot chillies added to it.
The spicy flavour comes from the salsa which garnishes
each nacho chip.
Makes 48

INGREDIENTS

4 large ripe avocados
2 medium tomatoes, chopped
2 tbsp finely chopped red onion
1 small garlic clove, finely chopped or crushed
juice of 1–2 lemons
1/4–1/2 tsp ground cumin
1/4–1/2 tsp chilli powder
salt
48 nacho chips
90 g (3 oz) mild Cheddar cheese, grated
125 ml (4 fl oz) plain low-fat yogurt, fromage blanc (see
page 156), or crème fraîche
1/2 batch Fresh Tomato Salsa (see page 29)
radishes for garnish

PREPARATION

1 Cut the avocados in half, remove the stones, and
scoop out the flesh with a spoon. Mash the flesh
in a bowl with a wooden spoon, or use a pestle
and mortar. Add the chopped tomatoes and
continue to mash together.

2 Add the onion and garlic, with lemon juice,
cumin, chilli powder, and salt to taste. Cover the
guacamole and refrigerate until you are ready to
assemble the nachos.

3 Place the nacho chips on baking trays and
sprinkle with the grated cheese. Place in a
preheated 190°C (375°F, Gas 5) oven for
5–10 minutes, until the cheese melts.

4 Place a spoonful of guacamole on each chip, then
a little yogurt, fromage blanc, or crème fraîche,
and a spoonful of salsa. Garnish with radishes.

 The guacamole and salsa will keep for several hours in
the refrigerator. Place the guacamole in a tightly
covered container; the surface will turn a little darker
than the rest of the guacamole, but when stirred, it
will regain its pale green colour.

VARIATION

GUACAMOLE & TOMATO NACHOS: Arrange *chopped*
tomato and avocado on top of the guacamole instead
of the yogurt, fromage blanc, or crème fraîche,
and the salsa. Garnish the nachos with *fresh*
coriander instead of radishes.

CHICKEN NACHOS WITH SALSA VERDE

Makes 48

INGREDIENTS

1 medium onion, coarsely chopped
2 garlic cloves, crushed
1.5 litres (2 1/2 pints) water
salt and freshly ground pepper
4 large chicken breasts, total weight
about 625 g (1 1/4 lb)
1/2 tsp dried thyme
1/2 tsp dried oregano or marjoram
2 bay leaves
1 batch Green Tomatillo Salsa (see page 47)
4 tbsp chopped fresh coriander
48 nacho chips
175 ml (6 fl oz) crème fraîche, fromage blanc
(see page 156), or plain low-fat yogurt
1 large or 2 small avocados, peeled, stoned, and diced
juice of 1 large lime
additional coriander leaves for garnish

PREPARATION

1 Place the onion, garlic, water, and 1 tsp salt in a
large, heavy-based saucepan and bring to a boil.
Add the chicken. Skim off any foam that rises,
then add the thyme, oregano or marjoram, and
the bay leaves. Reduce the heat, cover partially,
and simmer for 15 minutes.

2 Remove from the heat and let the chicken cool in
the broth. Remove the chicken from the broth,
and then skin, bone, and shred the meat.

3 Strain the stock through a muslin-lined sieve and
set aside for another purpose if desired.

4 Toss the shredded chicken with the tomatillo
salsa, chopped fresh coriander, and salt and
pepper to taste.

5 Place 1 heaped tsp of the mixture on each nacho
chip, and top with a little crème fraîche, fromage
blanc, or yogurt.

6 Toss together the diced avocado and lime juice,
and add salt to taste. Place about 2 tsp of the
mixture on top of each nacho chip, and garnish
with fresh coriander.

SUSHI ROLLS

Sushi rolls are a delight. They look beautiful and are delicious. The only specialist items you will need are a bamboo rolling mat, a wooden rice paddle (although conventional wooden spoons can be used), Japanese-style rice, and *nori* or dried seaweed.

★

CALIFORNIA SUSHI

This is a fresh variation of the classic Japanese sushi.
Makes about 70 slices

INGREDIENTS

375 g (12 oz) Japanese-style short-grain rice
4 tbsp seasoned rice vinegar (see page 156)
125 ml (4 fl oz) water mixed with 1 tbsp rice vinegar
(for dipping paddle or spoons, and hands)
8 sheets nori *seaweed*
2–3 ripe but firm avocados, peeled, cut into 5-mm (¼-in)
wide strips, and tossed in juice of ½ lemon
24 peeled, cooked prawns, cut in half lengthways,
then crossways

PREPARATION

1 Make the vinegared rice: rinse the rice until the water runs clear. Leave to soak in a saucepan for 15 minutes.

2 Cover the pan tightly and bring to a boil. Simmer for 5–10 minutes, until the rice hisses at the bottom of the pan. Do not uncover. Turn off the heat and let stand, covered, for 30 minutes.

3 Transfer the rice to a wide bowl and toss, using a flat, wooden rice paddle or 2 wooden spoons, until cool. When no more steam rises from the rice, gradually fold in the seasoned vinegar, 1 tbsp at a time. Dip the paddle or spoons in the water and vinegar mixture so that the rice does not stick to them. Cover the rice with a damp tea towel until ready to use. Do not refrigerate.

4 If the *nori* sheets are green, they have been toasted already. If they are black, toast them by fanning them over an open flame or a hot burner, until just bright green. This happens in seconds.

5 Place each *nori* sheet, shiny-side down, on a bamboo rolling mat. Moisten a measuring spoon with the water and vinegar mixture and spread 4–5 tbsp of the rice on each sheet (see page 85).

6 Lay the avocado strips along the middle of the rice and cover with pieces of prawn. Roll up the *nori* around the filling as directed on page 85, then cut each roll into 2-cm (¾-in) slices.

CUCUMBER SUSHI

This traditional sushi roll is known as kapa maki *in Japanese.*
Makes about 70 slices

INGREDIENTS

375 g (12 oz) Japanese-style short-grain rice
4 tbsp seasoned rice vinegar (see page 156)
125 ml (4 fl oz) water mixed with 1 tbsp rice vinegar
(for dipping paddle or spoons, and hands)
8 sheets nori *seaweed*
1–2 tsp wasabi *(Japanese horseradish paste)*
4 tsp sesame seeds, lightly toasted
90 g (3 oz) sliced pickled ginger
1 cucumber, seeded and cut into 5-mm
(¼-in) wide strips

PREPARATION

1 Make the vinegared rice and prepare the *nori* as directed in steps 1–5 of California Sushi, left.

2 Spread ⅛–¼ tsp wasabi in a line along the middle of the rice on each sheet of *nori*.

3 Sprinkle ½ tsp sesame seeds over each line of *wasabi*. Arrange some pickled ginger and cucumber strips side-by-side on top of the sesame seeds.

4 Roll up the *nori* around the cucumber and ginger filling as directed on page 85, then cut each roll into 2-cm (¾-in) slices.

TRADITIONAL SUSHI

Sushi is a popular Japanese snack based on rice flavoured with rice vinegar and shaped into balls, squares, or rolls. Traditionally, the rice is wrapped around a filling of raw fish or vegetables seasoned with a fiery horseradish paste called wasabi. *Pickles are added, then the whole is rolled in thin sheets of* nori *or dried seaweed. Sushi is fun — and healthy. Apart from the filling, the seaweed itself is a good source of vitamins and minerals.*

EAST MEETS WEST
*A platter of California Sushi — Japanese
rice rolls with a West-coast accent — is
garnished with Pickled Ginger Roses
(see page 155) on Cucumber
Fences (see page 154).*

FILLING & ROLLING NORI

Nori

Wasabi

1 Spread the rice on a nori sheet in a
5-mm (1/4-in) layer. Leave a
2.5-cm (1-in) margin at the top and
bottom. Place the filling on the rice.

2 Lift up the mat and nori and fold
them away from you over the filling.
Press down and roll up the nori, lifting
the mat as you go to avoid rolling it in.

A FEAST FROM THE ORIENT

Throw your own mini Oriental banquet with Japanese sushi, Chinese crispy spring rolls, Vietnamese soft spring rolls, and Indonesian saté, served with dipping sauces. Crown it all with a refreshing Oriental fruit platter of exotic tropical fruits.

Bottled hoisin sauce

Soy sauce sprinkled with sesame seeds

California Sushi (page 84) with prawns and pickled ginger

Oriental Fruit Platter (page 132)

Coconut Tuiles (page 127)

Soft Spring Rolls (pages 90–93) and Crispy Spring Rolls (page 94)

Chicken Saté (page 98)

WONTONS

Deep-fried or poached, wontons make irresistible party food. Spinach and tofu are two of my favourite healthy ingredients for the fillings, but you can also use any of the spring roll fillings (see pages 92–93).

★

SPINACH & TOFU WONTONS

This recipe is for deep-fried wontons. To poach, drop about 10 wontons at a time into 2 litres (3¹/₂ pints) boiling chicken or vegetable stock and poach for about 4 minutes, until al dente. *Serve hot or cold on cocktail sticks.*
Makes 40

INGREDIENTS

375 g (12 oz) fresh spinach, stalks removed, leaves washed, or 300 g (10 oz) packet frozen spinach, defrosted, excess moisture squeezed out
salt
1 tbsp sunflower, rapeseed, or peanut oil, more for deep frying
6 spring onions, both white and green parts, chopped
1 large garlic clove, finely chopped or crushed
1 tsp grated fresh root ginger
250 g (8 oz) firm tofu, cut into small dice
2 tbsp sesame seeds
2–3 tbsp soy sauce
2 tsp dry sherry
4 tbsp chopped fresh coriander
40 wonton wrappers
1 egg, beaten, or 1 tbsp cornflour or arrowroot
dipping sauce of your choice (see right and page 94)

PREPARATION

1 If using fresh spinach, blanch the spinach in boiling salted water for 1–2 minutes. Alternatively, put the spinach in a dry non-stick frying pan with only the water left on the leaves after washing. Toss over high heat for 1–2 minutes, until wilted.
2 Rinse the spinach under cold water, squeeze dry in a tea towel, and chop.
3 Heat the oil in a large non-stick frying pan, add the spring onions, garlic, and ginger, and stir-fry for 3 minutes, until the spring onions soften.
4 Add the diced tofu and sesame seeds, and stir-fry for 3–5 minutes over medium-high heat.
5 Add the spinach and stir-fry for another minute. Add the soy sauce and sherry, and continue to stir-fry over medium heat for 5 minutes.

6 Increase the heat, and cook, stirring, until all the liquid evaporates. Remove from the heat, and stir in the coriander. Taste, and adjust seasonings.
7 Finely chop the mixture either by hand or for just a second or two in a food processor. Fill the wontons as directed on page 89, sealing them with the beaten egg, or the cornflour or arrowroot dissolved in a little water.
8 Pour oil into a wok or deep-fat fryer up to a depth of 10 cm (4 in) and heat to 180°C (350°F). Deep-fry the wontons 6 at a time until golden brown. Remove with a slotted spoon and drain on paper towels. Let the oil reheat to 180°C (350°F) between each batch. Serve hot with a dipping sauce of your choice.

Quick Dipping Sauce

This sauce goes particularly well with wontons, but you can serve them with any of the dipping sauces on page 94.

Combine *125 ml (4 fl oz) water* with *4 tbsp each soy sauce and sake or dry sherry* and heat to boiling point. Stir in *4 tsp finely chopped or grated fresh root ginger*, and, if you prefer, *1 small red chilli, cored, seeded, and finely chopped.*

CHINESE PARCELS

Wontons are small Chinese dumplings made of paper-thin pastry, filled with a chopped or minced mixture of meat, seafood, or vegetables. You could make your own wonton wrappers from a dough of flour, salt, water, and egg, rolled out to wafer thinness, but it is easier to buy fresh or frozen ready-made wonton wrappers, which are available from Chinese food shops. If you cannot buy wonton wrappers, use two or three layers of filo pastry squares (see pages 142–143).

Once made, wontons are very versatile and take well to deep-frying, poaching, or steaming. They are usually served with a chilli and garlic or some other spicy sauce.

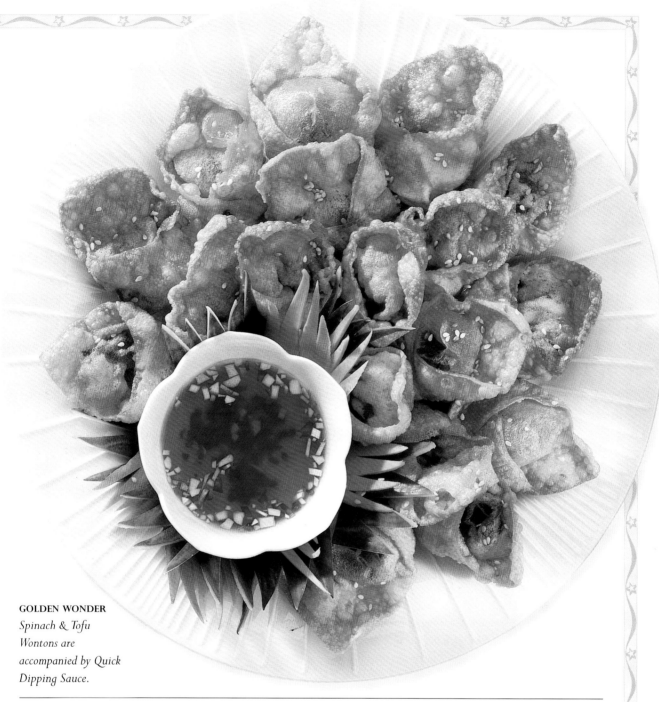

GOLDEN WONDER
*Spinach & Tofu
Wontons are
accompanied by Quick
Dipping Sauce.*

FILLING WONTONS

*1 Place 1 tsp of filling in the middle
of a wonton wrapper. Brush the
edges with beaten egg, or the cornflour
or arrowroot and water mixture.*

*2 Fold the wrapper diagonally over the
filling to form a triangle. Press
down the edges together firmly to seal.*

*3 Join the two bottom ends of the
triangle together at their tips and
seal. Repeat with the remaining
wrappers and filling.*

SOFT SPRING ROLLS

These are very fresh rolls made with rice-flour wrappers that need no cooking, just a quick soak to soften them. They are lighter than the deep-fried Crispy Spring Rolls (see page 94), and much healthier. There are two sizes of rice-flour wrappers available at Oriental specialist shops; I use the small ones for parties.

TO MAKE SOFT SPRING ROLLS

1 Prepare your choice of filling from the recipes given on pages 92–93.

2 Place 1 x 15-cm (6-in) rice-flour wrapper at a time in a bowl of hot water for about 30 seconds, until just softened.

3 Using 1 heaped tbsp of filling for each wrapper, make up each roll as directed below. Refrigerate, covered, until ready to serve.

4 Arrange the spring rolls on a large platter as illustrated here and garnish with carrot flowers (see page 155), radish roses and spring onion curls (see page 149), chopped fresh coriander, and finely chopped radish and carrot. Serve with a dipping sauce (see pages 88 and 94), if you prefer.

SUBTLE DIFFERENCES
Light and fresh, Vegetarian Soft Spring Rolls (see page 93) contain crunchy vegetables, such as green pepper, spring onion, carrot, and bean sprouts, which contrast with the soft wrapper.

FILLING & ROLLING A SOFT SPRING ROLL

1 *Place the filling in the middle of the rice-flour wrapper, slightly nearer to the edge closest to you.*

2 *Fold the sides of the wrapper over the filling, then roll the wrapper up tightly around the filling.*

Bean sprouts

Garlic

Spring onion

Ginger

Oil

Carrot

Chinese mushroom

Cellophane noodles

Green
pepper

Coriander

Soy sauce

Rice
vinegar

Salt

FILLINGS FOR SOFT SPRING ROLLS

I choose ingredients with contrasting textures and colours to fill these spring rolls. They complement the soft translucent wrappers beautifully. All the fillings can be made a day in advance and kept chilled.

★

CRUNCHY TOFU

To fill 20–25 x 15-cm (6-in) rice-flour wrappers

INGREDIENTS

8 medium Chinese dried mushrooms
2 tbsp grated fresh root ginger
2 tbsp peanut or rapeseed oil
12 spring onions, white and green parts, chopped
2 garlic cloves, finely chopped or crushed
250 g (8 oz) firm tofu, cut into small dice
2 tbsp soy sauce
1 tbsp dry sherry
250 g (8 oz) carrots, shredded
1/2 medium head green cabbage, shredded
175 g (6 oz) bean sprouts, chopped
1 red pepper, cored, seeded, and finely chopped
30 g (1 oz) fresh coriander, chopped

PREPARATION

1 Soak the mushrooms in boiling water for 30 minutes, until tender. Rinse in several changes of water, and squeeze dry. Cut away the stalks and discard. Cut the caps into thin slivers.
2 Stir-fry the ginger in the oil for 30 seconds, or until the ginger just begins to colour. Add the spring onions and stir-fry until they begin to soften. Add the mushrooms, garlic, and tofu.
3 Stir-fry for 1–2 minutes, then add the soy sauce and sherry. Stir-fry for 1 minute, then add the remaining vegetables. Remove from the heat, and add the coriander. Taste, and adjust seasonings.

PRAWN & CORIANDER

This easy filling is particularly light and refreshing, and it requires no cooking if you use ready-cooked prawns – just combine all the ingredients together. To fill 20 x 15-cm (6-in) rice-flour wrappers

INGREDIENTS

60 g (2 oz) rice vermicelli
500 g (1 lb) prawns, cooked, peeled, deveined, and cut in half crossways
60 g (2 oz) fresh coriander, chopped
30 g (1 oz) fresh mint leaves, slivered
8 medium Cos lettuce leaves, washed, dried, and shredded
4 tbsp lime juice
1 tbsp sesame oil
2–3 tsp grated fresh root ginger
soy sauce or salt
freshly ground pepper

PREPARATION

1 Soak the vermicelli in warm water for 20–30 minutes, until the noodles are tender. Drain and break them apart. Cut them into approximately 5-cm (2-in) pieces, with scissors.
2 Combine with the remaining ingredients. Adjust the soy sauce or salt to taste, and toss together.

SOFT SPRING ROLLS

Soft spring rolls are also known as Vietnamese spring rolls. Because the rice-flour wrapper is translucent, colourful filling ingredients clearly show through, which makes the rolls very appealing. Rice-flour wrappers are easy to work with and should be soaked in hot water before use to make them flexible when rolling. To prevent them drying out, it is best to work with one sheet at a time. Soft spring rolls are usually served cold, with a piquant dipping sauce to complement the filling. (See pages 88 and 94 for dipping sauce recipes.)

Fresh coriander

Fresh root ginger   **Tofu**

VEGETARIAN

*To keep the vegetables crunchy, make sure
not to overcook them.*
To fill 40–45 x 15-cm (6-in) rice-flour wrappers

INGREDIENTS

90 g (3 oz) cellophane noodles
1 litre (1³⁄4 pints) boiling water
8 medium Chinese dried mushrooms
250 g (8 oz) carrots
2 tbsp peanut or rapeseed oil
2 tbsp grated fresh root ginger
12 spring onions, both white and green parts, chopped
2 garlic cloves, finely chopped or crushed
1 green pepper, cored, seeded, and finely chopped
175 g (6 oz) bean sprouts, chopped
30 g (1 oz) fresh coriander, chopped
2 tbsp soy sauce
1 tbsp rice vinegar
salt and freshly ground pepper

PREPARATION

1 Put the cellophane noodles in a bowl and
pour on the boiling water. Let stand 30 minutes,
until tender.
2 While the noodles are softening, soak the
mushrooms. Place in a bowl and pour on boiling
water to cover. Let stand 30 minutes, until
tender. Drain, and rinse in several changes of
water. Squeeze dry. Cut away the stalks and
discard. Cut the caps into thin slivers.
3 Drain the noodles and cut into 2.5-cm (1-in)
lengths with scissors. Cut the carrots into
2.5-cm (1-in) matchsticks.
4 Heat half of the oil in a wok or a large, heavy-
based non-stick frying pan over medium heat
and add the ginger. Cook for about 30 seconds
until it just begins to colour, then add the spring
onions, garlic, and slivered mushrooms. Stir
together for 1 minute, and transfer to a bowl.
5 Add the remaining oil to the wok or frying pan
and heat over medium-high heat. Add the
carrots, green pepper, and bean sprouts. Stir
together for 2–3 minutes, until the vegetables
are crisp-tender. Add the noodles, coriander,
soy sauce, vinegar, and salt and pepper to taste.
Stir together and remove from heat. Taste, and
adjust seasonings.

SMOKED DUCK

You can put together this luscious filling in no time.
To fill 32 x 15-cm (6-in) rice-flour wrappers

INGREDIENTS

2 cucumbers
¹⁄2 tsp salt, plus salt for cucumber
2 tbsp rice vinegar
2 tbsp sesame oil
4 tbsp ready-made plum sauce
375 g (12 oz) smoked duck breast, cut into thin slivers
12 spring onions, both white and green parts, shredded
2 tbsp chopped fresh mint

PREPARATION

1 Shred the cucumbers, sprinkle liberally with salt,
and toss. Let stand in a sieve set over a bowl for
15 minutes. Rinse thoroughly, and squeeze dry.
2 Stir together the vinegar and ¹⁄2 tsp salt. When
the salt has dissolved, stir in the sesame oil and
half of the plum sauce.
3 Toss the slivers of duck breast with the remaining
plum sauce.
4 In a large bowl, combine the cucumber, plum
sauce and vinegar mixture, duck breast, spring
onions, and mint. Toss together well.

CRISPY SPRING ROLLS

These crispy Chinese rolls are surprisingly easy to make. Ready-made spring roll wrappers are available in Oriental food stores.

★

PORK OR CHICKEN CRISPY SPRING ROLLS

Makes 30–40 rolls

INGREDIENTS

3 tbsp soy sauce
1 tbsp sesame oil
1 tbsp water
1 tsp sherry
1/4 tsp sugar
salt and freshly ground pepper
375 g (12 oz) lean pork or chicken breast, or a combination, cut into thin slivers
2 tbsp peanut or rapeseed oil, more for deep-frying
2 tbsp grated fresh root ginger
12 spring onions, both white and green parts, chopped
2 garlic cloves, finely chopped or crushed
250 g (8 oz) mangetout, trimmed and cut into thirds
175 g (6 oz) bean sprouts, chopped
1 red pepper, cored, seeded, and finely chopped
30 g (1 oz) fresh coriander, chopped
1 tbsp rice vinegar
30–40 spring roll wrappers
1 tbsp arrowroot or cornflour
dipping sauce of your choice (see right)

PREPARATION

1 Mix together 1 tbsp of the soy sauce, the sesame oil, water, sherry, sugar, 1/4 tsp salt, and pepper to taste. Toss with the meat, and marinate for 30 minutes, stirring once or twice.

2 Heat half of the oil in a wok or heavy-based non-stick frying-pan over medium heat. Add the grated ginger. Stir-fry for 30 seconds, or until the ginger just begins to colour.

3 Add the spring onions, garlic, and the meat with its marinade. Stir-fry briefly, until the meat is cooked through. Transfer to a bowl.

4 Add the remaining oil to the pan and heat over medium-high heat. Stir-fry the mangetout, bean sprouts, and red pepper for 2–3 minutes, until the vegetables are crisp-tender.

5 Stir in the coriander, the remaining soy sauce, the rice vinegar, and salt and pepper to taste. Remove from the heat, and toss with the meat mixture. Taste, and adjust seasonings.

6 Place a spring roll wrapper diagonally on the work surface, so that it appears diamond-shaped in front of you rather than square. Place 1 tbsp filling on the wrapper, near the bottom corner.

7 Fold the sides in over the filling, then fold the bottom corner over this and roll up tightly away from you. Seal with the arrowroot or cornflour dissolved in a little water.

8 Fill a wok or deep-fryer with oil to a depth of 10 cm (4 in) and heat to 180°C (350°F). Deep-fry the rolls in batches until golden brown, turning them to brown them evenly (this should only take a couple of minutes). Remove and drain on paper towels. Let the oil heat back up to 180°C (350°F) after each batch. Serve with the dipping sauce of your choice.

These rolls are best served hot. If they have cooled before serving, reheat the oil to 180°C (350°F) and briefly crisp the rolls in the hot oil. The fillings can be made on the day before you make the rolls, but they will lose some texture.

Dipping Sauces

Serve wontons, soft spring rolls, and crispy spring rolls with either or both of these dipping sauces. Just combine all the ingredients in a bowl. You could also serve the Quick Dipping Sauce (see page 88), bottled hoisin or plum sauce for those who like sweet flavours, or soy sauce.

TERIYAKI SAUCE: Combine *4 tbsp tamari soy sauce, 4 tbsp sake or dry sherry, 2 tbsp mild honey, 1 tbsp grated fresh root ginger (or 1/2 tsp ground ginger), 2 finely chopped or crushed garlic cloves, 1 tbsp sesame oil,* and *1/4 tsp mustard powder.*

TAHINI-TAMARI SAUCE: Combine *4 tbsp tamari soy sauce, 125 ml (4 fl oz) sesame tahini, 1 tsp grated fresh root ginger, 2 tsp dry sherry,* and enough hot water to thin out the sauce to the desired consistency.

FISH, MEAT & POULTRY

In France, a buffet that features high-protein items, such as pâtés, fish, and chicken, is referred to as a buffet renforcé, one that is fortified with satisfying dishes. Meat and fish dishes add substance to a buffet, and this is important if it is likely to be the main meal for your guests. It's also a good idea to serve at least one high-protein item when people may be drinking alcohol over the course of a few hours.

UNDER THE GRILL

Grilled bite-sized food on skewers is a feature of many different cuisines – for example, Middle-Eastern kebabs and Mediterranean brochettes. Fish, seafood, lean meat and poultry, and vegetables can all be threaded on to skewers and then either grilled or barbecued – the marinade will determine the accent. If grilling or barbecuing fish, use firm-fleshed, slightly oily fish, such as tuna and swordfish.

SAVOURY SKEWERS
Middle-Eastern Meatballs surround Chicken & Pepper Kebabs and Prawn & Baby Corn Kebabs, with Tahini-Yogurt Dip in a green pepper cup.

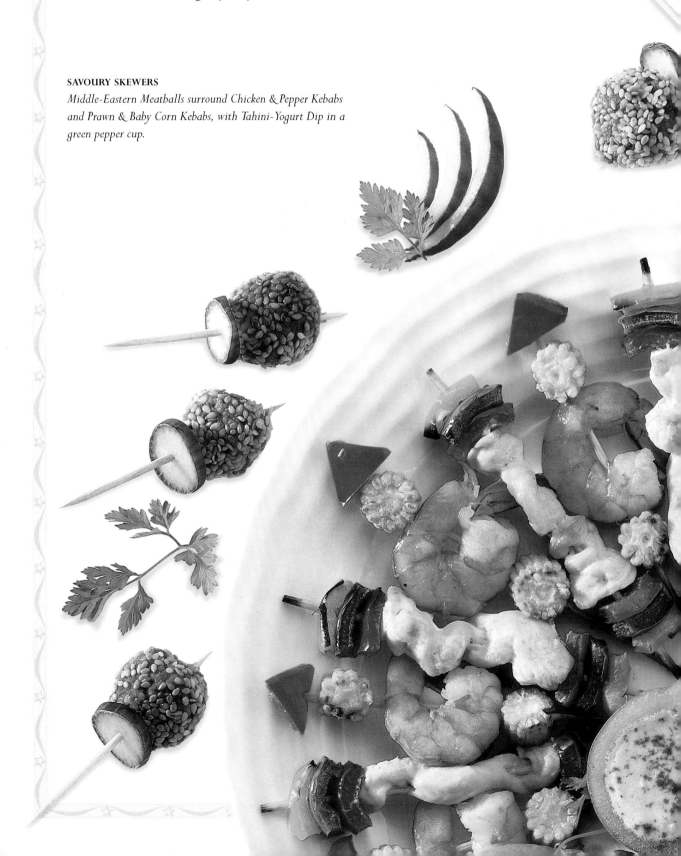

TO MAKE KEBABS OR MEATBALLS

1 Prepare meatballs (see page 99), or cut fish, meat, or poultry into strips or 2.5-cm (1-in) cubes, and toss in marinade according to recipe (see pages 98–99). Refrigerate for the time given in individual recipes. Stir the mixture from time to time to redistribute the marinade.

2 If making kebabs on wooden skewers, soak the skewers in warm water for at least 30 minutes before using, to prevent them from burning while grilling.

3 Thread the marinated ingredients on to skewers. Grill the kebabs or meatballs on a prepared outdoor barbecue, under a preheated grill, or in a preheated 190°C (375°F, Gas 5) oven for the time given in the recipe, basting every 2 minutes with the marinade. Serve with dipping sauces of your choice (see pages 28–29 and 99).

Middle-Eastern Meatballs

CHICKEN & PEPPER KEBABS

Makes about 25

INGREDIENTS

6 chicken breasts, skinned and boned
3 garlic cloves, peeled
salt and freshly ground pepper
seeds from 10 cardamom pods
1/2 tsp ground allspice
1/2 tsp ground cinnamon
1/2 tsp ground cumin
5 tbsp plain low-fat yogurt
juice of 3 large limes
3 tbsp olive oil
3 medium peppers (red, yellow, and green),
cored, seeded, and cut into 2-cm (3/4-in) squares

PREPARATION

1 Cut the chicken into 2.5-cm (1-in) pieces and place in a bowl.
2 Pound the garlic with 1/4 tsp salt in a pestle and mortar. Grind the cardamom seeds in a spice grinder (or pound in a pestle and mortar), and add to the garlic with the other spices and 1/4 tsp ground pepper. Mix together with the yogurt, lime juice, and olive oil.
3 Add the marinade to the chicken and stir well. Refrigerate for at least 2 hours, stirring occasionally.
4 Thread the chicken on to about 25 x 12-cm (5-in) skewers, with pepper squares at either end. Cook on a barbecue or under a preheated grill for 4–6 minutes, or in a preheated 190°C (375°F, Gas 5) oven for 5–10 minutes, basting every 2 minutes with the marinade.
5 Serve with any dip of your choice (see page 99).

VARIATIONS

PRAWN & BABY CORN KEBABS: Substitute *1 kg (2 lb) tiger prawns, peeled and deveined,* for the chicken and *20 baby corn, cut into 1-cm (1/2-in) pieces* for the green and yellow peppers. Halve the red pepper squares into triangles. Marinate the prawns for 30 minutes only. Thread 1 prawn between 2 baby corn pieces and finish with a red pepper triangle. Grill for 2 minutes, turning often. Serve hot or cold.

PRAWN & PEPPER KEBABS: Substitute *1 kg (2 lb) tiger prawns, peeled and deveined,* for the chicken. Cut *1 green and 1 yellow pepper* into 2.5-cm (1-in) pieces. Marinate the prawns for 30 minutes. Thread prawns and peppers on to skewers and grill for 2 minutes. Serve sprinkled with *chopped parsley.*

BEEF & CHICKEN SATE

You can make these Indonesian-style kebabs with all chicken
or all beef, if you prefer not to mix the two meats together.
Makes about 25

INGREDIENTS

250 g (8 oz) tender beef steak
250 g (8 oz) skinned and boned chicken breast
FOR THE MARINADE
2 tbsp soy sauce
1 tbsp white wine vinegar
1 tbsp sunflower or rapeseed oil
1 tsp ground coriander
1 tsp ground cumin
1 tsp chilli powder
1 tsp ground ginger
1 tsp sugar
FOR THE PEANUT SAUCE
1 1/2 tbsp sunflower or rapeseed oil
175 g (6 oz) natural peanuts, crushed
2 garlic cloves, finely chopped
1/2 tsp crushed dried red chillies
1 tsp ground ginger
1 tsp brown sugar
salt
1 tbsp lemon juice
350 ml (12 fl oz) chicken stock
about 2 tbsp fine dried white breadcrumbs

PREPARATION

1 Cut the steak and chicken into strips, and mix well with all the marinade ingredients. Let stand for at least 3 hours, but not longer than 12 hours.
2 Make the peanut sauce: heat the oil in a heavy-based pan over medium-high heat and stir-fry the dry ingredients until browned. Stir in the lemon juice and chicken stock, and reduce slightly. Add sufficient breadcrumbs to thicken. Let cool.
3 Thread the steak and chicken strips separately on to about 25 x 12-cm (5-in) presoaked saté sticks. Grill on a barbecue or under a preheated grill for 2–3 minutes on each side. Serve hot, with the peanut sauce.

SOAK & COOK

It is important to marinate raw fish, meat, poultry, and seafood before it is grilled. The marinade not only adds flavour, it also has a tenderizing effect because of its acid content. Do not marinate fish in a lemon or lime marinade for more than 2 hours, or it will begin to "cook" in the acid.

TUNA & RED PEPPER KEBABS WITH GINGER-SOY MARINADE

Seasoned with a pungent, Japanese-style marinade, these delicate kebabs need no sauce, just a squeeze of lime or lemon if you like.
Makes about 25

INGREDIENTS

4 tbsp soy sauce
2 tbsp rice vinegar
2 tbsp sunflower or rapeseed oil
2 tbsp water
1 tbsp dark sesame oil
1/4 tsp sugar
3 spring onions, both white and green parts, finely chopped
2 garlic cloves, finely chopped or crushed
2 tbsp grated fresh root ginger
2 tbsp finely chopped lemon grass
500 g (1 lb) fresh tuna, cut into 2·5-cm (1-in) cubes
1 medium red pepper, cored, seeded, and cut into 1-cm (1/2-in) squares

PREPARATION

1 Put the soy sauce, rice vinegar, sunflower or rapeseed oil, water, sesame oil, and sugar in a large bowl, and whisk together. Add the spring onions, garlic, ginger, and lemon grass, and combine well.

2 Add the tuna and toss together. Cover and marinate, in or out of the refrigerator, for 30 minutes, stirring occasionally. Stir in the red pepper after the first 15 minutes.

3 Thread the pieces of tuna and pepper on to about 25 presoaked small skewers, allowing 2 pieces of tuna to 1 piece of red pepper. Arrange the skewers on a baking tray.

4 Place the baking tray under a preheated grill, 12–15 cm (5–6 in) from the heat. After 1 minute, turn the skewers over and baste the fish with the marinade. Grill another minute, and remove from the heat. The fish should be pink on the inside. Serve hot.

Suggested Dipping Sauces

- *Quick Dipping Sauce (see page 88)*
- *Teriyaki Sauce (see page 94)*
- *Tahini-Tamari Sauce (see page 94)*

MIDDLE-EASTERN MEATBALLS

Makes 100–120 small meatballs

INGREDIENTS

175 g (6 oz) fine- or medium-grain bulgur wheat
1 large white onion, chopped
salt and freshly ground pepper
500 g (1 lb) minced lamb or beef
1/2–1 tsp ground cinnamon
1/2–1 tsp ground cumin
2 tbsp water
4 tbsp sesame seeds, toasted
750 g (1 1/2 lb) courgettes, cut into 5-mm (1/4-in) slices and sautéed lightly
Tahini-Yogurt Dip (see page 29)

PREPARATION

1 Soak the bulgur wheat in cold water for about 15 minutes.

2 Meanwhile, place the onion with 1 tsp salt in a food processor fitted with the metal blade and blend to a coarse purée. Remove and set aside.

3 Place the meat in the food processor and process until smooth and pasty. Add the onion and salt mixture, and cinnamon, cumin, and pepper to taste. Work together until evenly mixed, then, while the machine is running, add the water. The mixture should still be smooth and pasty.

4 Drain the bulgur wheat and squeeze out any excess water. Add to the meat mixture and process again until smooth.

5 Moisten your hands and form the meat mixture into small balls, about 2-cm (3/4-in) in diameter. The mixture will be sticky, but workable.

6 Place the meatballs on a baking tray and grill under a preheated grill, about 10–12.5 cm (4–5 in) from the heat, for 2 1/2–3 minutes.

7 Spread the toasted sesame seeds on a board and roll the meatballs over them to coat. Thread cocktail sticks with a meatball and a slice of courgette. Serve with Tahini-Yogurt Dip or any dip of your choice (see left).

VARIATION

SPICY MEATBALLS: Use *1 tsp ground cumin*, and add *1 tsp paprika* to the mixture. You could also add *ground allspice, more black pepper*, and *a few cloves of finely chopped garlic*.

A Mexican Fiesta

Create a festive mood with the vibrant flavours and vivid colours of these Mexican recipes. Piquant dips and toppings served with nacho chips or crunchy chicory leaves are complemented by fresh and chocolate-coated fruit.

Chicken Nachos with Salsa Verde *(page 83)*

Ceviche on chicory leaves *(page 104)*

Fresh Tomato Salsa (page 29) with nacho chips (page 81)

Mexican Fruit Platter (page 132)

Guacamole (page 83) with nacho chips

MARINATED FISH

Tartares and ceviches make delicate hors d'oeuvre. Serve them on bread, crackers, or vegetable wafers – their fresh flavours go well with them. Ceviche can also be served on chicory leaves or on nacho chips.

★

MUSSELS ON THE HALF SHELL

This is a beautiful way to present mussels. First they are steamed, then tossed in a sauce, and finally, they are set back in their shells. The sauce you choose will determine the nature of the dish: if you choose a salsa, the dish will have a Mexican character, while the other sauces will give the mussels a Mediterranean flavour.
Serves 10–12

INGREDIENTS

2 litres (3¹/₂ pints) fresh mussels
4 tbsp salt or vinegar
250 ml (8 fl oz) dry white wine
250 ml (8 fl oz) water
2 shallots or 1 onion, chopped
4 garlic cloves, crushed
600 ml (1 pint) Fresh Tomato Salsa (see page 29),
Tomato Concassée (see page 72), Basil Pesto (see page 25),
or Coriander Pesto (see page 25)
fresh coriander, parsley, or basil for garnish (depending on your choice of sauce)

PREPARATION

1 Brush the mussels and scrape off any barnacles; pull out the beards. Discard any with cracked shells or any that do not close when tapped.
2 Place in a bowl and rinse in several changes of cold water. Cover with cold water and stir in the salt or vinegar. Let stand for 15 minutes. Drain, rinse, and soak again for another 15 minutes. Drain and rinse again.
3 Combine the wine, water, shallots or onion, and garlic in a large saucepan and bring to a boil. Add the mussels, cover, and steam for 5 minutes, shaking the pan or stirring halfway through to redistribute the mussels.

4 Remove the pan from the heat and strain the cooking liquid through a muslin-lined sieve into a bowl. Set aside.
5 Remove the mussels from their shells, discarding any that have not opened, and set half of the shells aside. Rinse the mussels quickly.
6 In a large bowl, mix together the sauce of your choice with 250 ml (8 fl oz) of the cooking liquid strained from the mussels. Toss the mussels with this mixture, cover, and let marinate in the refrigerator for 1 hour or longer.
7 To serve, place the mussels on the reserved shells and spoon on some sauce. Arrange on a platter and garnish with fresh herbs.

You cannot speed up cleaning the mussels, because each one of them must be inspected to make sure it closes when tapped. However, you can save time by buying prepared salsa, tomato sauce, or pesto for the marinade.
The cooked mussels can be refrigerated in the marinade for up to 24 hours.

VARIATION

CLAMS ON THE HALF SHELL: Substitute *1.5 litres (2½ pints) clams* for the mussels.

Fresh Fish

The most important thing to consider when you are serving raw or marinated fish is the quality of the fish itself. Uncooked fish must be impeccably fresh. Buy from a reputable fishmonger, and only on the day you wish to serve it. To be extra sure, particularly about salmon, ask the fishmonger if the fish has been fresh-frozen – parasites cannot survive in fish that has been frozen for 72 hours. Do not buy the fish unless you are absolutely sure of this.

FISH TARTARE

Fish tartare is minced raw fish tossed with a sauce. Here I use horseradish sauce, but you can also use any of the others suggested below.
Serves 12–15

INGREDIENTS

500 g (1 lb) centre-cut tuna fillet, dark meat and connective tissue removed,
or salmon fillet, skin and small bones removed
2 shallots, finely chopped
2 tbsp capers, drained and rinsed
1 ripe but firm avocado, peeled, stoned, and diced very fine (optional)
4 tbsp lemon or lime juice
1 tsp Worcestershire sauce
salt and freshly ground pepper
FOR THE HORSERADISH SAUCE
3 tbsp grated fresh horseradish,
or 1¹/₂–2 tbsp prepared horseradish
4 tbsp fromage blanc (see page 156) or soured cream
2 tbsp sherry vinegar
2 tbsp olive oil
2 tbsp water
1 tsp soy sauce
salt and freshly ground pepper
FOR SERVING
24 crostini (see page 69), pitta triangles, or thin slices of cucumber
chopped fresh herbs and herb sprigs, such as chives, parsley, chervil, and dill
lemon or lime wedges

PREPARATION

1 Mince the fish in a food processor, or chop it very finely with a sharp knife. Do not purée. Toss with the shallots, capers, avocado (if using), lemon or lime juice, Worcestershire sauce, and salt and pepper to taste.
2 Make the horseradish sauce by combining all the ingredients in a blender or whisking together in a bowl, until smooth.
3 Toss the fish in the sauce, cover, and let marinate in the refrigerator for about 1¹/₂ hours.
4 To serve, either transfer to an attractive bowl and surround with crostini, pitta triangles, or cucumber slices, or use as a topping for canapés. Garnish with chopped fresh herbs and herb sprigs, and lemon or lime wedges.

VARIATIONS

Substitute the Horseradish Sauce with *Coriander Pesto (see page 25), Asian Sesame-Ginger Dip (see page 29),* or *Mustard Sauce (see Gravadlax, page 104).*

MARINATED RAW FISH ON COCKTAIL STICKS

Small squares of marinated tuna or salmon may be served as mini-brochettes on cocktail sticks, as illustrated below. Sliced pickled ginger is available at Oriental food shops.
Serves 10

INGREDIENTS

500 g (1 lb) centre-cut tuna fillet, dark meat and connective tissue removed,
or salmon fillet, skin and small bones removed
salt and freshly ground pepper
1 tbsp soy sauce
1 tbsp rice vinegar or balsamic vinegar
2 tbsp mirin (Japanese sweet rice wine), or 2 tsp sugar
2.5-cm (1-in) piece of fresh root ginger, grated
90 g (3 oz) sliced pickled ginger
2 tsp water
4–5 spring onions, white parts only, sliced thickly on the diagonal
dipping sauce of your choice

PREPARATION

1 Cut the fish into 1-cm (¹/₂-in) cubes. Place in a bowl and toss with salt and pepper to taste.
2 Mix together the soy sauce, vinegar, mirin or sugar, ginger, and water, and toss with the fish. Cover, and let marinate in the refrigerator for 30 minutes to 1 hour.
3 Thread the fish, pickled ginger, and spring onion slices on wooden cocktail sticks.
4 Serve with Horseradish Sauce (see Fish Tartare), Coriander Pesto (see page 25), Asian Sesame-Ginger Dip (see page 29), or Mustard Sauce (see Gravadlax, page 104).

Marinated Raw Fish on Cocktail Sticks with Horseradish Sauce

CEVICHE

Ceviche is a Latin-American dish of marinated raw fish. The fish, in fact, is no longer raw when you eat it, because the lime juice "cooks" it during marinating.
Serves 12–15

INGREDIENTS

750 g (1 1/2 lb) very fresh fish fillets, such as cod, whiting, red snapper, or bream;
or the same weight centre-cut tuna fillet, dark meat and connective tissue removed;
or 750 g (1 1/2 lb) shelled scallops
350–500 ml (12–16 fl oz) lime juice (about 7 large limes)
1 small onion, sliced
2 garlic cloves, finely chopped or crushed
1–2 fresh or canned jalapeño or serrano peppers, seeded and chopped
2 medium tomatoes, chopped
1 large or 2 small ripe avocados, peeled, stoned, and diced
2–4 tbsp olive oil
salt and freshly ground pepper
4–5 tbsp chopped fresh coriander
small lettuce or chicory leaves, or 24 crostini (see page 69) or nacho chips (see page 81) for serving

PREPARATION

1 Cut the fish or scallops into 1-cm (1/2-in) cubes and place in a bowl. Pour on the lime juice and toss together well. Cover and refrigerate.

2 Marinate white fish or scallops for 7 hours, tossing every once in a while. Marinate tuna for about 1 1/2 hours or a little longer. It should remain pink in the middle.

3 Add the onion, garlic, peppers, tomatoes, and avocado, then add olive oil, and salt and pepper to taste. Toss together, cover, and refrigerate for another hour.

4 Remove from the refrigerator, and stir in the coriander, adding more to taste if you prefer. Adjust seasonings. Let stand for 15–30 minutes.

5 Before serving, place the ceviche in a colander set over a bowl, and drain off most of the marinade.

6 Serve on small lettuce or chicory leaves, or on crostini or nacho chips. If you prefer, you can serve all of the ceviche on a platter or in a salad bowl, encircled by lettuce or chicory leaves.

GRAVADLAX

The Scandinavian classic, gravadlax, sometimes also called gravlax, is sugar-and-salt-cured salmon. Although it needs 4 days to marinate, it is well worth the wait.
Serves 12–15

INGREDIENTS

2 x 500 g (1 lb) centre-cut salmon fillets, skin left on
3 tbsp coarse sea salt
3 tbsp sugar
2 tbsp vodka or aquavit
1 tbsp black peppercorns, crushed in a pestle and mortar
45 g (1 1/2 oz) fresh dill, chopped
cucumber slices and pumpernickel bread for serving
lemon or lime wedges and dill sprigs for garnish
FOR THE MUSTARD SAUCE
125 ml (4 fl oz) sunflower or rapeseed oil
125 ml (4 fl oz) plain low-fat yogurt
4 tbsp coarse-grained mustard
4 tbsp lime juice
salt and freshly ground pepper

PREPARATION

1 Score each salmon fillet on the skin side, making several diagonal cuts about 3 mm (1/8 in) deep.

2 Combine the salt and sugar, and sprinkle 5 tsp over the bottom of a large glass or earthenware baking dish.

3 Place 1 salmon fillet, skin-side down, in the dish. Sprinkle with half of the vodka or aquavit, then sprinkle with the peppercorns. Sprinkle with 4 tsp of the salt and sugar mixture, and spread half of the dill over the fillet in an even layer.

4 Rub 4 tsp of the remaining salt and sugar mixture over the flesh side of the remaining fillet. Place this, skin-side up, on top of the first fillet. Rub the remaining salt and sugar mixture over the skin.

5 Cover the salmon with a sheet of waxed paper, then some foil. Place a flat surface, such as a chopping board, on top and weigh down with 1.5–2.5 kg/3–5 lb cans of food or weights.

6 Refrigerate for 48 hours. Check after 5–6 hours, and drain any liquid that has accumulated in the dish. Check again every 12 hours. Turn the salmon and chill for another 48 hours, turning twice.

7 In the meantime, just before serving, make the mustard sauce: whisk together all the ingredients, with salt and pepper to taste. Cover, and refrigerate.

8 To serve the gravadlax, remove the skin, and cut the fish into very thin slices. Sprinkle with the dill and serve on cucumber slices or pieces of pumpernickel, with the mustard sauce, lemon or lime wedges, and dill sprigs.

FISH ON A DISH

Translucent slices of delicate Gravadlax are served on cucumber rounds and pumpernickel slices, and garnished with Mustard Sauce, lemon or lime wedges, and sprigs of dill. A bowl of Mustard Sauce is served alongside.

CARPACCIO

Carpaccio is paper-thin slices of raw beef, salmon, or tuna. It is often accompanied by a pungent sauce and is delicious served on crostini (see page 69), pitta bread, cheese biscuits, or thin wafers of vegetables.

★

BEEF CARPACCIO

This is the classic carpaccio, dressed with olive oil and lemon and traditionally served with rocket leaves and shavings of Parmesan cheese (as illustrated on page 60).
Serves 8–10

INGREDIENTS

3 x 125-g (4-oz) pieces of filet mignon *beef*
4 tbsp olive oil
4 tbsp lemon juice
rocket leaves
18–24 crostini (see page 69)
salt and freshly ground pepper
18–24 Parmesan Shavings (see page 154) for garnish

PREPARATION

1 Wrap each piece of beef in foil, and place in the freezer for 1–2 hours, until just about to freeze.
2 Whisk together the olive oil and lemon juice.
3 Remove the beef from the freezer, unwrap, and slice paper-thin. Flatten the slices by pounding them between 2 pieces of parchment paper.
4 Cut the slices into 3.5-cm (1½-in) pieces. Tear the rocket leaves into pieces and place a piece on each crostini. Top with a piece of beef and drizzle on a little of the olive oil and lemon dressing. Sprinkle with salt and pepper and garnish with the Parmesan shavings.

VARIATION

BEEF CARPACCIO ROLLS: Cut *375 g (12 oz) beef carpaccio* into strips 2.5 cm (1 in) wide and 5 cm (2 in) long. Place *½–1 tsp Horseradish Sauce* at one end of each beef strip, or spread it evenly along the strip, and gently roll up the strip. Serve on *croûtons,* or *daikon (Japanese radish) slices,* or spear the rolls with cocktail sticks.

--- *Sauces for Carpaccio* ---

• *Coriander Pesto (see page 25)*
• *Horseradish Sauce (see page 103)*
• *Asian Sesame-Ginger Dip (see page 29)*
• *Mustard Sauce (see page 104)*

SALMON CARPACCIO

Serves 8–10

INGREDIENTS

500 g (1 lb) salmon fillet
sauce of your choice (see below)
18–24 crostini (see page 69)
salt and freshly ground pepper

PREPARATION

1 Skin, wrap, and freeze the salmon as directed in steps 1 and 2 on page 107.
2 Prepare your chosen sauce.
3 Remove the salmon from the freezer and slice as directed in step 3 on page 107.
4 Spread each crostini with a little sauce, then top with sliced salmon. Season to taste, arrange on a platter, and garnish as desired.

VARIATIONS

TUNA CARPACCIO: Substitute *500 g (1 lb) centre-cut tuna steak fillet, dark meat and connective tissue removed,* for the salmon.
TUNA CARPACCIO ROLLS: Coriander Pesto (see page 25) goes very well with Tuna Carpaccio. Cut *500 g (1 lb) Tuna Carpaccio* into strips 2.5 cm (1 in) wide and 5 cm (2 in) long. Place *1 tsp pesto* at one end of each tuna strip, or spread it evenly along the strip, and gently roll up the strip. Serve on *croûtons,* or *cucumber slices,* or spear the rolls with cocktail sticks.

**CARPACCIO
PLATTER**
*Rows of Tuna
Carpaccio alternate
with rows of Salmon
Carpaccio, both on crostini.*

PREPARING SALMON CARPACCIO

*1 Grasp the salmon skin at the tail
end and, with a sawing action, work
a sharp chef's knife between the skin
and the flesh, from the tail end.*

*2 Roll and wrap the skinned salmon
fillet tightly in foil. Chill in the
freezer for 10–15 minutes, until just
about to freeze.*

*3 Unwrap the chilled salmon and slice
as thinly as possible. Squeeze the
slices between parchment paper with
your fingers, and cut to fit the crostini.*

Pâtes & Terrines

Traditionally served as hors d'oeuvre, pâtés and terrines may be some of the most elaborate and time-consuming recipes to prepare, but they are well worth the extra effort and attention. Their rich, meaty textures and flavours add substance to a party spread and you will find that a little goes a long way. Rather than serving my terrines whole, I prefer to cut them into dainty slices and serve them on different-shaped canapés, while I spread the pâtés on tiny canapés and garnish them prettily to make them as appealing as possible.

MEATY CANAPES

Mounds of rich Brandied Liver Pâté (right) on triangular canapés are garnished with slices of baby gherkin, a dab of sun-dried tomato paste, and parsley.

Brandied Liver Pâté

Duck Terrine

POTTED DUCK

Slices of Duck Terrine (above) are served on floral-shaped canapés. They are garnished with fans made from baby gherkin sliced lengthways and topped with a dab of sun-dried tomato paste and parsley.

Brandied Liver Pâté

TO MAKE PATE & TERRINE CANAPES

1 Cut thick slices of bread into an assortment of attractive shapes with pastry cutters. Toast until light golden on both sides.

2 Cut thin slices from terrines and cut the slices with a pastry cutter or into smaller slices to fit the canapés. Alternatively, set terrines in ramekins or other small moulds, unmould, and cut slices lengthways.

3 Arrange the slices of terrine on the canapés and garnish as desired.

4 For Brandied Liver Pâté canapés, simply spread the pâté, smooth into a neat shape, and garnish as desired.

Duck Terrine

SEE-THROUGH SLICES
Star-shaped canapés make a delicate base for slices of Lamb Terrine en Gelée, the colourful ingredients showing through the light jelly (right). A dab of sun-dried tomato paste and a sprig of dill top the garnish of crossed blanched turnip bâtons.

Lamb Terrine en Gelée

PATES & TERRINES

Pâtés are a smooth mixture of finely minced meat, often set with butter. They can be served sliced or spread on canapés. Terrines are more elaborate: different meats or vegetables are layered either with a mixture of minced meat or a meat or poultry jelly. To appreciate their intricate layers, serve them sliced.

★

BRANDIED LIVER PATE

This is a luxurious-tasting pâté that is extremely quick and simple to put together with the help of a food processor.
Serves 10

INGREDIENTS

6 tbsp butter
1 large shallot, sliced
500 g (1 lb) chicken livers
1/2 tsp salt
5 whole black peppercorns
2 tsp fresh thyme leaves, or 1 tsp dried thyme
3 tbsp brandy (or Madeira, sherry, or Armagnac)

PREPARATION

1 Melt half of the butter over medium-high heat in a frying pan and add the shallot. Fry gently, stirring, for about 1 minute.

2 Add the chicken livers. Cook, stirring, until the centres of the livers are faintly pink. Do not allow the livers or the shallots to brown. Remove from the heat and let the livers cool in the juices in the pan.

3 Transfer the contents of the pan, including the pan juices, to a food processor fitted with the metal blade. Add the salt, peppercorns, and thyme, and purée until smooth.

4 With the machine running, add the brandy, then the remaining butter, a little at a time. Continue to purée until the mixture is smooth.

5 Transfer to a ramekin or other serving dish. Cover well and chill. The pâté should have the spreading consistency of semi-firm butter.

The pâté will keep for 5 days in the refrigerator. Bring to room temperature before serving.

DUCK TERRINE

Start making this terrine well in advance: you will need a day for marinating the meat (during which time you should make the stock for the demi-glace), and the cooked terrine should sit in the refrigerator for 3–5 days or even up to a week before serving, to let the flavours ripen.
Serves 15–20

INGREDIENTS

FOR THE TERRINE
1 1/2 medium ducks to yield:
2 whole duck breasts, total weight 250 g (8 oz)
and 1 kg (2 lb) boned duck meat (not breast meat),
skin, fat, and tendons removed, cut into 2-cm (3/4-in) cubes
500 g (1 lb) chicken livers
375 g (12 oz) fresh pork belly fat, diced
2 x 2.5-cm (1-in) pieces of orange peel
3 tbsp whole coriander seeds, ground
1 1/2–2 tbsp salt
1 tbsp sugar
2 tsp dried thyme
2–2 1/2 tsp freshly ground pepper
1 tsp grated fresh root ginger
3/4 tsp ground cinnamon
1/2 tsp ground cloves
1/2 tsp ground bay leaves
2 pinches of freshly grated nutmeg
90 ml (3 fl oz) dry white wine
125 ml (4 fl oz) brandy
2 tbsp butter or duck fat (from the underside
of the duck skin)
90 g (3 oz) shallots, finely chopped (to make
4 tbsp when cooked)
2 tbsp cornflour
125 ml (4 fl oz) crème fraîche or double cream
1 garlic clove, finely chopped or crushed
2 eggs, beaten
175 ml (6 fl oz) duck demi-glace (see page 111)
75 g (2 1/2 oz) pig's caul,
or 250 g (8 oz) thinly sliced fresh pork fat,
for lining the terrine
60 g (2 oz) shelled pistachios, peeled (optional)

FOR THE STOCK AND DEMI-GLACE

1¹/₂ tbsp butter

1 duck carcass, cut up

2 medium carrots, chopped

1 medium onion, quartered

3 litres (5 pints) water, or to cover

2 x 2.5-cm (1-in) slices of orange peel

*1-cm (¹/₂-in) piece of fresh root ginger,
peeled and thinly sliced*

*1 bouquet garni, made with 3 sprigs each of parsley and
coriander, 2 bay leaves, and 2 sprigs of thyme*

5-mm (¹/₄-in) piece of cinnamon stick

¹/₂ piece of star anise

1 tsp salt

1 tsp peppercorns

¹/₂ tsp Szechwan pepper

PREPARATION

THE FIRST DAY

1 Wrap the whole duck breasts in greaseproof or parchment paper and refrigerate.

2 Combine the remaining duck meat with the chicken livers and pork fat. Add the orange peel, coriander, salt, sugar, thyme, pepper, ginger, cinnamon, cloves, bay, and nutmeg.

3 Heat the wine briefly in a saucepan, remove from the heat, and set alight. When the flames die down, cool and stir into the meat mixture, with the brandy. Mix, cover, and refrigerate for 24 hours. Stir often to distribute the flavours.

4 Meanwhile, make the stock, which will be reduced for the demi-glace. Melt the butter in a large saucepan over medium heat and brown the cut-up carcass, carrots, and onion for about 5 minutes, stirring constantly.

5 Add the water and the remaining ingredients and bring to a simmer. Skim. Cover, reduce the heat, and simmer for 2 hours, skimming from time to time, until the stock is richly flavoured, but not too salty. Strain through a muslin-lined sieve.

6 Return the stock to the saucepan, bring to a boil, and reduce to 175 ml (6 fl oz). Remove the demi-glace from the heat and let cool. Refrigerate overnight.

THE NEXT DAY

7 Mince the meat mixture twice, in small batches, through the large cutting disc of a meat mincer, or in a food processor fitted with the metal blade, using the pulse action.

8 Melt 1 tbsp butter (or the equivalent amount of duck fat) in a small frying pan over medium-low heat. Add the shallots, and cook, stirring, for about 5 minutes, until tender. Stir into the meat mixture, with the cornflour, crème fraîche or cream, garlic, eggs, and demi-glace.

9 Cut the duck breasts lengthways into 1-cm (¹/₂-in) wide strips. Season lightly with salt and pepper. Melt the remaining 1 tbsp butter or duck fat in a heavy-based frying pan over medium-high heat. Brown the strips on all sides for about 5 minutes. They should be cooked through but slightly pink.

10 Line a heavy, lidded 1.5-litre (2¹/₂-pint) terrine mould with the pork caul or slices of pork fat, leaving enough overhanging to cover the top of the terrine. If the pieces are not large enough for this, set aside a sufficient quantity to cover the top of the terrine later.

11 Fill with one-quarter of the meat mixture. If using pistachios, sprinkle in half of them in an even layer. Cover with a quarter of the meat mixture. Lay strips of duck breast lengthways over the meat mixture in a single layer. Cover with a quarter of the meat mixture. Sprinkle on the remaining pistachios, and if there are any remaining strips of duck breast, lay them on top.

12 Cover with the remaining meat mixture (don't worry if the meat goes over the rim, it will reduce in volume as it cooks). Fold the overhanging caul or pork fat over the terrine, and cover tightly with the lid.

13 Tap the mould squarely on the work surface once, to get rid of any air pockets. Place in a roasting tin and fill with water. Place in the lower half of a preheated 160°C (325°F, Gas 3) oven, and bake for 2–2¹/₂ hours, until a meat thermometer reads 70°C (160°F) when inserted three-quarters of the way down in the middle. Let cool, then refrigerate for 3–7 days before serving.

LAMB TERRINE EN GELEE

This is a light, simple terrine that is very attractive when
unmoulded, because the ingredients show through the
gelée or jelly which holds them together.
Slices are even prettier, with the colourful pieces of
the vegetables showing through.
Serves 12

INGREDIENTS

FOR THE GELEE

500 g (1 lb) lamb bones
2 medium carrots, coarsely chopped
1 large leek, cleaned and coarsely chopped
4 sprigs of basil or chervil
4 sprigs of parsley
3 bay leaves
2 cloves
1 tbsp coriander seeds
1 tbsp peppercorns
1.5 litres (2¹/₂ pints) water
1¹/₂ tbsp gelatine powder
salt and freshly ground pepper

FOR THE TERRINE

2 tbsp butter
3 medium carrots, cut into 5-mm (¹/₄-in) dice
875 g (1³/₄ lb) lamb, cut into 1-cm (¹/₂-in) dice
1 large bouquet of basil or chervil sprigs
(whichever used for the gelée)
150 g (5 oz) green beans, trimmed
2 medium turnips, peeled
and cut into 5-mm (¹/₄-in) thick strips
1 small red pepper, cored, seeded,
and finely diced
30 g (1 oz) fresh basil or chervil
(whichever used for the gelée), chopped

PREPARATION

1 Make the gelée: combine all the ingredients, except for the gelatine and salt and pepper, in a large saucepan, and bring to a boil. Skim the surface with a large spoon to remove any froth. Cover, and cook over medium heat for 2 hours or longer, skimming occasionally, until you have a rich, aromatic broth.

2 Strain into a bowl through a muslin-lined sieve and return the broth to the pan. Bring to a boil, and simmer until the broth is reduced to 750 ml (1¹/₄ pints).

3 Bring the broth to a boil again and stir in the gelatine powder until it dissolves. Remove from the heat. Add salt and pepper to taste (the cold gelée requires plenty of seasoning for the flavours to emerge).

4 In the meantime, while the broth is cooking, prepare the ingredients for the terrine: melt half of the butter over low heat in a flameproof casserole and add the carrots. Cook, stirring occasionally, for 10 minutes. Add the remaining butter and the lamb, and cook, stirring, until the lamb has browned. Add the herb bouquet.

5 Cover, and place in a preheated 150°C (300°F, Gas 2) oven for 2 hours, stirring every 15 minutes. Remove from the oven, and reduce any remaining liquid. Season with salt and pepper. Remove the herb bouquet.

6 Bring a large pan of water to a boil, add 1 tsp salt, and the green beans. Cook for 5 minutes, until tender. Remove from the pan with a slotted spoon and refresh under cold water. Add the turnips to the boiling water and cook for 5–10 minutes, until tender. Drain and refresh under cold water. Set aside.

7 If the gelée has set, heat gently to liquefy. Stir in the red pepper. Add half of the herbs to the gelée and half to the meat mixture. Spoon enough gelée into a 1-litre (1³/₄-pint) terrine mould to cover the bottom by 1 cm (¹/₂ in). Place in the freezer for a few minutes to set.

8 Remove the mould from the freezer and add a layer of half of the meat mixture. Pour on enough gelée to cover. Place in the freezer again for a few minutes to set.

9 Remove the mould from the freezer and add a layer of green beans. Cover with gelée, and place in the freezer again for a few minutes.

10 Repeat with the turnips and the remaining meat, ending with a layer of gelée. (You can also arrange the meat and vegetables in several alternating layers if you wish, pouring on gelée to cover each layer.)

11 Cover the mould and place in the refrigerator for at least 3 hours, or until set.

12 To unmould, run a sharp knife between the edges of the terrine and the mould, then dip the mould in hot water for no more than 1 minute, to loosen the gelée. Invert a plate or platter over the top of the terrine, and flip over. If the terrine does not unmould, dip again briefly in hot water: be careful not to immerse for too long, or the gelée at the sides will melt and destroy the shape of the terrine.

DESSERTS

A selection of desserts is the climax of any party
— and they always look colourful. A fresh fruit platter
served with creamy dips, or petits fours, might be all
that is necessary. On the other hand, you might want
to offer cakes and pastries together with fruit. The
fruit tartlets or the choux puffs filled with coffee
cream are always sensational, while chocolate-coated
fruit and chocolate bouchées will provide a
luxurious finishing touch to any meal.

DESSERT TARTLETS

Bite-sized tartlets are easy to make and the basic tartlet shell is extremely versatile. You can serve prebaked and cooled pastry shells filled with a choice of fruit on a bed of Crème Pâtissière (see page 153) or cream cheese as shown here. For baked tartlets, fill partially baked pastry shells from the choice of fillings given on pages 116–119, and bake through.

FRESH FRUIT TARTLETS

Makes 16 x 5-cm (2-in) tartlets
or 10 x 7-cm (3-in) tartlets

INGREDIENTS

250 g (8 oz) cream cheese
2 tbsp plain low-fat yogurt
2 tbsp sugar
2 tsp finely grated lemon zest
2 tsp lemon juice
16 x 5-cm (2-in) or 10 x 7-cm (3-in) tartlet shells made
with Almond Dessert Pastry, baked and cooled
(see pages 140–141)
mixed fresh fruit of your choice (see below)
200 g (7 oz) apricot jam

PREPARATION

1 In a food processor fitted with the metal blade, blend together the cream cheese, yogurt, sugar, lemon zest, and lemon juice.
2 Divide the cream cheese mixture evenly between the tartlet shells and smooth the tops.
3 Arrange the fruit of your choice decoratively on top of the cream cheese filling, cutting them into halves, quarters, or slices to fit as necessary.
4 Melt the jam in a saucepan. Work through a sieve, then quickly brush over the fruit while the glaze is still warm, taking care not to disturb your arrangement.

A CORNUCOPIA OF FRUIT

A selection of fresh fruit to fill tartlets can include raspberries, blueberries, strawberries, clementines, mandarins, cherries, figs, kiwi fruit, and mangoes.

Fresh Fruit Tartlets

BAKED TARTLETS

The fillings in these tartlets are baked in their pastry shells. Use unbaked or partially-baked Pâte Sucrée or Almond Dessert Pastry (see pages 140–141), or Rough Puff Pastry (see page 139) for the shells. Instead of making individual tartlets, you can also make a large 25-cm (10-in) tart.

★

LEMON TARTLETS

Makes 24 x 5-cm (2-in) or 16 x 7-cm (3-in) tartlets

INGREDIENTS

165 ml (5½ fl oz) lemon juice
125 g (4 oz) sugar
2 tbsp plain low-fat yogurt or crème fraîche
4 eggs
24 x 5-cm (2-in) or 16 x 7-cm (3-in) tartlet shells, baked blind and cooled (see pages 139–141)

PREPARATION

1 Whisk together the lemon juice and sugar. Add the yogurt or crème fraîche and combine well.
2 Beat the eggs into the mixture, one at a time.
3 Pour the custard mixture into the tartlet shells. Bake tartlets in a preheated 190°C (375°F, Gas 5) oven for about 15 minutes or until the custard has set.

VARIATION

LIME TARTLETS: Substitute *165 ml (5½ fl oz) lime juice* for the lemon juice and *2 tbsp soured cream* for the crème fraîche.

RHUBARB & HONEY TARTLETS

Makes 24 x 5-cm (2-in) or 16 x 7-cm (3-in) tartlets

INGREDIENTS

500 g (1 lb) rhubarb, cut into 1-cm (½-in) pieces
4 tbsp mild honey, such as lavender, acacia, or clover
1–2 tbsp sugar
1 tbsp Grand Marnier (optional)
24 x 5-cm (2-in) or 16 x 7-cm (3-in) unbaked tartlet shells (see pages 139–141)
whipped cream for decoration
strawberries, halved lengthways, for decoration

PREPARATION

1 Combine the rhubarb, honey, and 1 tbsp sugar in a non-corrosive saucepan and bring to a boil over medium heat. Reduce the heat to medium-low, cover, and simmer for 10 minutes, stirring occasionally, until the rhubarb is tender.
2 Increase the heat and cook for 10–15 minutes, stirring, until the rhubarb mixture holds its shape.
3 Let cool, then taste, and add more sugar if you prefer. Stir in the Grand Marnier, if using.
4 Spoon the mixture into the tartlet shells, and bake in a preheated 200°C (400°F, Gas 6) oven for 10 minutes. Reduce the heat to 180°C (350°F, Gas 4) and bake for a further 10 minutes.
5 Let cool and decorate with piped whipped cream, and strawberry halves.

Rhubarb & Honey
Tartlets in Rough Puff
Pastry shells

Using Rhubarb

Rhubarb is a vegetable, but because it is extremely sour, it is sweetened considerably when cooked and therefore treated as a fruit. It makes a delicious partner for pastry and is often served with other fruit, especially oranges and strawberries.

Rhubarb must be handled cautiously. Its leaves contain oxalic acid and can be poisonous: always discard them before cooking.

Take care while cooking rhubarb as it tends to splutter. To avoid being burned, use a long-handled spoon.

To test if the cooked rhubarb will set for Rhubarb & Honey Tartlets, pour a little of the mixture on to a plate that has been chilled in the freezer for about 10 minutes. The rhubarb should hold its shape and not spread over the plate.

Rhubarb stalks

117

RICH PECAN SQUARES

*Here, a pecan tart is baked in a rectangular tin,
then cut into small squares.*
Makes 1 x 25- x 30-cm (10- x 12-in) tart

INGREDIENTS

*1 x 25- x 30-cm (10- x 12-in) partially baked tart shell
made with Pâte Sucrée (see pages 140–141)*
60 g (2 oz) unsalted butter
125 ml (4 fl oz) mild honey
3 large eggs
1 tbsp rum
1 tsp vanilla extract (see page 156)
1/2 tsp salt
1/4 tsp freshly grated nutmeg
250 g (8 oz) broken pecans

PREPARATION

1 Partially bake the tart shell in a preheated 190°C
(375°F, Gas 5) oven for 5 minutes.
2 Cream the butter with the honey. Beat the eggs
into the butter and honey mixture, one at a time.
3 Stir in the rum, vanilla extract, salt, and nutmeg.
Fold in the pecans.
4 Pour the mixture into the partially baked shell,
and bake in a preheated 190°C (375°F, Gas 5)
oven for 35–40 minutes, until a knife inserted in
the centre comes out clean.
5 Remove from the oven and let cool. Cut into
3.5–5-cm (1½–2-in) squares.

VARIATION

WALNUT SQUARES: Substitute *maple syrup* for the
honey, *brandy* for the rum, and *chopped walnuts* for
the pecans.

Rich Pecan Squares

APRICOT & ALMOND TARTLETS

Makes 24 x 5-cm (2-in) or 16 x 7-cm (3-in) tartlets

INGREDIENTS

250 g (8 oz) dried apricots
150 g (5 oz) blanched skinned almonds, finely chopped
1/4 tsp almond extract (see page 156)
*24 x 5-cm (2-in) or 16 x 7-cm (3-in) partially baked
tartlet shells (see pages 139–141)*

PREPARATION

1 Place the apricots in a bowl and pour on boiling
water to cover. Let stand for 1 hour or longer.
2 Drain the apricots and, if you prefer, dice into
5-mm (1/4-in) pieces. Place in a bowl and add the
almonds and almond extract and mix together.
3 Divide the filling evenly among the partially
baked tartlet shells and bake in a preheated
200°C (400°F, Gas 6) oven for 15–20 minutes.

MINCEMEAT TARTLETS

Makes 36 x 5-cm (2-in) tartlets

INGREDIENTS

1 seedless orange, including peel, cut into pieces
finely grated zest of 1 lemon
125 ml (4 fl oz) apple juice
2 large cooking apples, peeled and finely diced
175 g (6 oz) sultanas or raisins
90 g (3 oz) chopped dates
125 g (4 oz) brown sugar
1/4 tsp ground cinnamon
1/4 tsp ground cloves
1/4 tsp freshly grated nutmeg
1/8 tsp salt
2 tbsp rum
1/4 tsp vanilla extract
*36 x 5-cm (2-in) partially baked tartlet shells
(see pages 139–141)*

PREPARATION

1 Blend the orange, lemon zest, and apple juice to a
purée in a food processor fitted with the metal
blade. Heat in a non-corrosive pan over low heat.
Stir in the apples, sultanas, dates, sugar, spices, and
salt. Cover and simmer for 15 minutes, stirring
occasionally. Remove from the heat and stir in the
rum and vanilla.
2 Divide the filling evenly among the partially
baked tartlet shells and bake in a preheated
190°C (375°F, Gas 5) oven for 20 minutes.

CHERRY CLAFOUTIS TARTLETS

Makes 24 x 5-cm (2-in) or 16 x 7-cm (3-in) tartlets

INGREDIENTS

750g (1½ lb) fresh cherries, stalks and stones removed
3 tbsp kirsch
6 tbsp sugar
3 large eggs
1 vanilla bean, or ½ tsp vanilla extract (see page 156)
100 g (3½ oz) plain flour, sifted
175 ml (6 fl oz) plain low-fat yogurt
pinch of salt
24 x 5-cm (2-in) or 16 x 7-cm (3-in) partially baked tartlet shells (see pages 139–141)

PREPARATION

1 Toss the cherries with the kirsch and 2 tbsp of the sugar in a bowl. Let stand for 30 minutes.
2 Drain the liquid from the cherries and beat together with the eggs, the seeds from the vanilla bean or the vanilla extract, and the remaining sugar.
3 Slowly beat in the flour. Add the yogurt and salt. Mix together well.
4 Arrange a few cherries in each partially baked tartlet shell. Pour in the batter.
5 Bake in a preheated 200°C (400°F, Gas 6) oven for 25 minutes, or until the tops are browned and the filling firm. Cool on racks.

 The tartlets will keep for several hours at room temperature.

VARIATIONS

APRICOT CLAFOUTIS: Substitute *apricots, blanched, peeled, halved, and stoned,* for the cherries. You can use *canned apricots in syrup* in winter. Place an apricot half in each tartlet shell, either unsliced or sliced down to the base and fanned out. Pour on the batter and bake as above.

GRAPE CLAFOUTIS: Substitute *seedless grapes* for the cherries. Place as many as will fit in each tartlet shell, pour on the batter, and bake as above.

BLACKBERRY OR RASPBERRY CLAFOUTIS: Substitute *blackberries* or *raspberries* for the cherries. Place as many as will fit in each tartlet shell, pour on the batter, and bake as above.

BLUEBERRY OR REDCURRANT CLAFOUTIS: Substitute *blueberries* or *redcurrants* for the cherries. Place as many as will fit in each tartlet shell, pour on the batter, and bake as above.

CRANBERRY-PEAR TARTLETS

These are beautiful tartlets for a Christmas party, with sliced pears fanned around festive cranberry sauce.
Makes 24 x 5-cm (2-in) or 16 x 7-cm (3-in) tartlets

INGREDIENTS

175 ml (6 fl oz) orange juice
2 tbsp cornflour
125 g (4 oz) sugar
300 g (10 oz) cranberries
2 tbsp finely grated orange zest
3 large Comice pears, peeled, cored, and thinly sliced
(cut slices to fit the size of the tartlet shells if they are too large)
2 tbsp lemon juice
24 x 5-cm (2-in) or 16 x 7-cm (3-in) partially baked tartlet shells (see pages 139–141)
2 tbsp apricot jam

PREPARATION

1 Combine the orange juice, cornflour, and all but 2 tbsp of the sugar in a large saucepan. Add half of the cranberries and bring to a boil, stirring. Remove from the heat and stir in the remaining cranberries and the orange zest. The mixture should be quite thick. Set aside.
2 Toss the pear slices in a bowl with the remaining sugar and the lemon juice. Arrange them, overlapping, in a circle in the partially baked tartlet shells, reserving any juice. Place 1 tbsp of the cranberry sauce on top. Bake in a preheated 200°C (400°F, Gas 6) oven for 20 minutes.
3 Meanwhile, make a glaze: melt the jam in a saucepan with any reserved pear juice.
4 Remove the tartlets from the oven and brush with the glaze. Cool on racks before serving.

VARIATION

CHOCOLATE PEAR TARTLETS: Divide *125 g (4 oz) plain chocolate, broken into small pieces,* between the tartlet shells. Whisk together *1 egg* with *150 ml (¼ pint) single cream.* Add *2.5-cm (1-in) piece of stem ginger, finely chopped.* Pour into the tartlet shells. Arrange *2 pears, peeled, cored, and sliced,* in the tartlet shells. Bake in a preheated 200°C (400°F, Gas 6) oven for 20 minutes.

Choux Puffs

These feathery puffs can be filled simply with Crème Pâtissière (see page 153), with a coffee-flavoured filling (see below) or with fresh fruit and Chantilly cream as illustrated here. Unfilled choux puffs freeze well. To defrost and crisp, transfer them from the freezer to a preheated 220°C (425°F, Gas 7) oven for about 4 minutes.

★

COFFEE CREAM PUFFS

Makes 40 puffs

INGREDIENTS

250 ml (8 fl oz) milk
1 1/2 tbsp ground coffee
3 egg yolks
75 g (2 1/2 oz) caster sugar
4 tbsp plain flour, sifted
a little chilled butter
175 ml (6 fl oz) whipping cream
1 tbsp icing sugar, more for dusting
40 choux puffs (see page 138), baked and cooled

PREPARATION

1 Scald the milk. Add the coffee and infuse for 20 minutes or longer. Strain the mixture through a double layer of muslin.
2 Beat the egg yolks and sugar together until thick and lemon-coloured. Whisk in the flour.
3 Slowly add the flavoured milk to the egg yolk mixture, whisking constantly. Transfer to a heavy-based saucepan and stir constantly with a whisk or wooden spoon over medium heat, until the mixture thickens. Pour into a bowl.
4 Rub the surface of the coffee cream lightly with a piece of chilled butter, or place a piece of greaseproof paper directly over the surface, so that the cream does not form a skin. Let cool.
5 Whip the cream until it forms stiff peaks, adding icing sugar. Add 2 tbsp of the whipped cream to the coffee cream and whisk together well to lighten the mixture. Fold in the remaining whipped cream.
6 Remove the tops of the choux puffs and fill the bottoms with the coffee cream, as directed in steps 1 and 2 on page 121. Dust the lids lightly with icing sugar and replace on the choux puffs.

FRESH FRUIT & CREAM PUFFS

Fresh fruit is tucked into a bed of Chantilly cream in the filling for these choux puffs. To enrich the Chantilly cream, add a flavouring to the whipped cream with the icing sugar. Vanilla, brandy, rum, or a liqueur are all good choices.
Makes 40 puffs

INGREDIENTS

600 ml (1 pint) whipping cream
3 tbsp icing sugar, more for dusting
40 choux puffs (see page 138), baked and cooled
250 g (8 oz) apricots, halved, stoned, and thinly sliced
3 kiwi fruit, peeled and sliced
200 g (7 oz) wild strawberries
200 g (7 oz) blueberries
mint leaves for decoration

PREPARATION

1 To make the Chantilly cream, pour the whipping cream into a chilled bowl and whip with a whisk or electric mixer until soft peaks form. Add the icing sugar, and whip until the cream forms soft peaks again and just holds its shape.
2 Remove the tops of the choux puffs and fill the bottoms with the Chantilly cream and fruit, as directed on page 121. Dust the lids lightly with icing sugar, replace on the choux puffs, and decorate with mint leaves.

WILD & WONDERFUL

Wild strawberries, also called alpine strawberries and fraises des bois, are renowned for their aromatic flavour, reminiscent of roses. The small, dark red berries grow to about 1 cm (1/2 in) long and do not need to be hulled. European varieties of cultivated strawberries are all derived from fraises des bois, but none equal their tantalizing flavour.

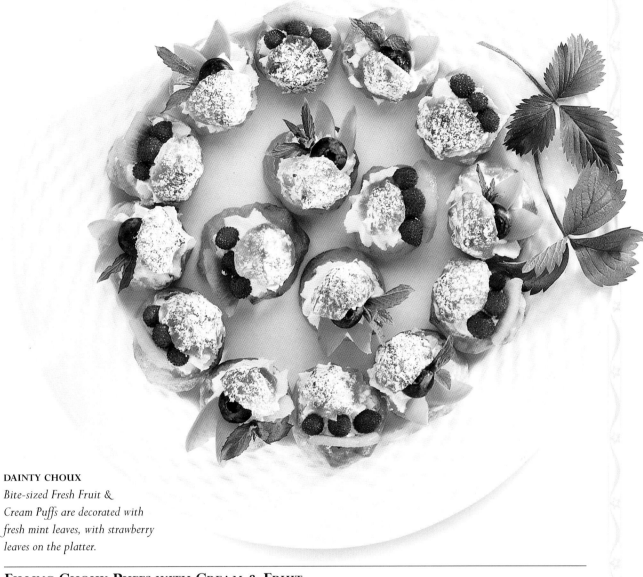

DAINTY CHOUX

*Bite-sized Fresh Fruit &
Cream Puffs are decorated with
fresh mint leaves, with strawberry
leaves on the platter.*

FILLING CHOUX PUFFS WITH CREAM & FRUIT

1 Using a sharp knife, carefully cut off the top from each choux puff and reserve to use as lids.

2 Fill a piping bag fitted with a star nozzle with Chantilly cream, and pipe into the bottoms of the puffs.

3 Gently press pieces of the prepared fruit into the Chantilly cream to make an attractive pattern on each puff.

CHOCOLATE DESSERTS

Few can resist chocolate – for many, it is the ultimate confection. Make your own delectable end-of-party collection from chocolate-coated fruit, brownies, and chocolate bouchées. Buy the best quality chocolate you can. The richest chocolate contains the highest percentage of cocoa solids: look for more than 60 per cent.

Chocolate-coated Fruit

Celebration Brownies

PARTY HIGHLIGHTS

Crown a party with chocolate desserts such as Chocolate-coated Fruit, Celebration Brownies, and chocolate bouchées.

*White Chocolate &
Orange Bouchées*

TO USE MELTED CHOCOLATE IN CHOCOLATE DESSERTS

• Dip fruit in melted chocolate (see page 124).

• Pipe melted chocolate on to Celebration Brownies (see page 124).

• Combine melted chocolate with whipped cream to fill chocolate shapes (see Dark Chocolate Bouchées, page 125).

*Dark Chocolate
Bouchées*

Coffee & Nut Bouchées

Mocha Bouchées

CELEBRATION BROWNIES

Moist and chewy brownies are usually made with chocolate, but can include butterscotch and vanilla. When decorated, they are perfect for special occasions. Brownies should be soft inside and crisp on the outside. Do not overbake them or they will be too dry.
Makes 25–30

INGREDIENTS

150 g (5 oz) plain chocolate, broken into small pieces
60 g (2 oz) unsalted butter, more for greasing
150 g (5 oz) plain flour, more for dusting
1/2 tsp baking powder
1/2 tsp salt
125 g (4 oz) caster sugar
2 large eggs
90 g (3 oz) shelled walnuts, chopped
60 g (2 oz) white chocolate for decoration (optional)

PREPARATION

1 Butter a 20-cm (8-in) square baking tin. Line it with greaseproof paper, butter the paper, and dust with flour.

2 Melt the chocolate and butter together in a bowl set over a pan of simmering water, stirring every 15 seconds. Remove from the heat just before fully melted and stir to complete the melting. Let cool to room temperature.

3 Sift the flour, baking powder, and salt into a bowl.

4 Beat the sugar and eggs together in another bowl until pale and thick. Stir in the flour mixture, melted chocolate, and chopped nuts, and combine well.

5 Transfer the batter to the prepared baking tin, and bake in a preheated 180°C (350°F, Gas 4) oven for 20–30 minutes, or until a cocktail stick inserted in the centre comes out with just a little batter on it. The brownies should still be moist in the centre when they are done.

6 Loosen the edges with a palette knife. Invert the tin on to a baking tray, and remove the tin and the lining paper. Place another tray that has been lightly greased over the brownies, then invert again and remove the top tray. Let cool, then cut into small squares, no more than 5 cm (2 in).

7 Melt the white chocolate, pour into a paper piping bag (see page 151), and pipe a decorative pattern on top of each brownie.

CHOCOLATE-COATED FRUIT

Almost any fruit can be dipped in chocolate and served as dessert, or you can serve a large platter of fruit set around a fondue pot full of melted chocolate. Supply cocktail sticks for dipping the fruit into the chocolate.
Makes about 50

INGREDIENTS

1 red apple
1 papaya
125 g (4 oz) cape gooseberries
125 g (4 oz) seedless green grapes
125 g (4 oz) plain chocolate, broken into small pieces

PREPARATION

1 Core the apple and cut it into about 12 wedges. Peel and halve the papaya, remove the seeds, and cut the flesh into about 15 wedges, depending on the size of the fruit.

2 Dry the cut fruit with paper towels so that the chocolate can set on it. Peel back the husks of the cape gooseberries to reveal the fruit but do not remove them.

3 Melt the chocolate as directed on page 150. Remove from the heat just before fully melted and stir to complete the melting.

4 Dip each piece of the fruit in the chocolate as directed on page 151 and place it on a baking tray lined with greaseproof paper. Place the tray in the refrigerator, to set the chocolate.

VARIATIONS

WHITE CHOCOLATE-COATED FRUIT: Substitute *125 g (4 oz) white chocolate* for the plain chocolate.

CHOCOLATE & NUT-COATED FRUIT: Spread *125 g (4 oz) chopped almonds or hazelnuts* on a flat surface. After dipping each piece of fruit in the melted chocolate, lightly roll the chocolate-coated part over the chopped nuts. Place the fruit on a baking tray lined with greaseproof paper and place the tray in the refrigerator, to set the chocolate.

LIQUEUR CHOCOLATE-COATED FRUIT: Stir in *1–2 tbsp liqueur of your choice, such as Grand Marnier or Cointreau,* into the melted chocolate before coating the fruit.

Chocolate-coated Strawberries

DARK CHOCOLATE BOUCHEES

*Chocolate cups or cases with creamy fillings look fantastic
and are relatively easy to prepare. Vary the shapes and
fillings as much as possible so your bouchées look
professionally made.*
Makes 24

INGREDIENTS

125 g (4 oz) plain chocolate, broken into small pieces
1 egg yolk
1 tbsp butter, softened
100 ml (3 1/2 fl oz) whipping cream
*24 chocolate cups, made with 125 g (4 oz) plain chocolate
(see page 150)*
white chocolate curls (see page 151) for decoration

PREPARATION

1 Melt the chocolate as directed on page 150.
When the chocolate has almost melted, add the
egg yolk and stir until the mixture is thick.
Remove from the heat.

2 Take the bowl from the pan and let the chocolate
mixture cool slightly. Stir in the softened butter
and let the mixture cool until it reaches room
temperature. It should still be creamy.

3 Meanwhile, whip the cream with a whisk or an
electric mixer until stiff peaks form. Cut and fold
the cream into the cooled chocolate mixture.

4 Fill the chocolate cups with the chocolate cream
(see page 150), and decorate with white
chocolate curls.

VARIATIONS

CREAMY CHOCOLATE & ORANGE BOUCHEES:
Substitute *a combination of 60 g (2 oz) white chocolate
and 60 g (2 oz) plain chocolate* for the 125 g (4 oz)
plain chocolate. Add *1 tbsp finely grated orange zest*
to the melted chocolate with the softened butter.

WHITE CHOCOLATE & ORANGE BOUCHEES:
Substitute *white chocolate* for the plain chocolate,
and *triangular chocolate cases* for the chocolate cups.
Decorate with *orange zest* instead of chocolate curls.

COFFEE & NUT BOUCHEES: Substitute *2 tbsp instant
coffee granules, dissolved in 2 tbsp boiling water,* for
the plain chocolate. Decorate with *macadamia
nuts dipped in a little melted plain chocolate,* instead
of chocolate curls. A *sprig of mint* can be used for
additional decoration.

MOCHA BOUCHEES: Fill *diamond-shaped chocolate
cases* with the filling used in the Coffee & Nut
Bouchées (see above). Decorate with a sprinkling
of *coffee essence* instead of chocolate curls.

CHOCOLATE TRUFFLES

*These irresistible chocolate balls can be made at least
2–3 days before serving.*
Makes about 30

INGREDIENTS

500 g (1 lb) plain chocolate, broken into small pieces
2 eggs
100 g (3 1/2 oz) caster sugar
200 g (7 oz) butter, softened
3 tbsp cocoa powder

PREPARATION

1 Melt the chocolate as directed on page 150.
Remove from the heat and add the eggs and
sugar, stirring vigorously until smooth. Return
to the heat and continue cooking over gentle heat
for 5 minutes, stirring constantly.

2 Remove the bowl from the pan and beat in the
butter, 1 tbsp at a time, until the mixture is
smooth and thick. Refrigerate for 2–3 hours
until firm.

3 Scoop out about 1 tsp of the chilled chocolate
mixture on to a cool work surface and, with your
hands dusted with cocoa powder, roll the
chocolate mixture into 3.5-cm (1 1/2-in) balls.

4 Roll each truffle in cocoa powder to coat it
completely, then place in a paper case.
Keep chilled until ready to serve.

VARIATIONS

NUT TRUFFLES: Toast *60 g (2 oz) shelled and skinned
whole hazelnuts* in a 180°C (350°F, Gas 4) oven for
about 5 minutes, until they are golden. Follow the
recipe for the Chocolate Truffles until the end of
step 2. Cover each hazelnut with the chocolate
mixture, roll into balls as in step 3, and continue
until the end of the recipe.

RUM TRUFFLES: Follow the recipe for the Chocolate
Truffles until the end of step 2, but do not
refrigerate. Add *4 tbsp dark rum* to the mixture and
continue until the end of the recipe.

ORANGE LIQUEUR TRUFFLES: Follow the recipe for
the Chocolate Truffles until the end of step 2, but
do not refrigerate. Add *3 tbsp orange liqueur, such as
Grand Marnier,* to the mixture and continue until
the end of the recipe.

PETITS FOURS

Petits fours are delectable little cakes and biscuits – traditionally baked at the end of the day in the *petit four,* the French for a small oven or at low heat. A selection of petits fours makes a decorative feature on a party table and are especially good to serve with fresh fruit, coffee, or liqueurs.

★

ALMOND BISCOTTI

Bite-sized biscotti make great finger food. The almond taste of these biscotti goes particularly well with sweet dessert wine or with espresso coffee.
Makes about 120

INGREDIENTS

125 g (4 oz) almonds
2 eggs
60 g (2 oz) caster sugar
60 g (2 oz) light brown sugar
1 tsp bicarbonate of soda
1/4 tsp salt
275 g (9 oz) wholemeal or plain flour, or a combination
1 egg white

PREPARATION

1 Scatter the almonds on a baking tray. Place the tray in a preheated 190°C (375°F, Gas 5) oven, and toast the almonds for about 10 minutes, until golden brown.
2 Remove from the oven and chop medium-fine with a knife (do not use a food processor because it will either grind the almonds or leave large chunks). Leave the oven on.
3 Butter and flour a baking tray. In a mixer, or food processor fitted with the metal blade, blend together the eggs and the sugars. Add the bicarbonate of soda and salt, then gradually work in the flour.

4 Scrape the dough out on to a lightly floured work surface. Press out the dough and scatter the toasted almonds over the top. Fold the dough over the toasted nuts and knead gently until they are evenly distributed through the dough. Add a little more flour if the dough is sticky.
5 Divide the dough into quarters, and shape each quarter into a long log, about 2 cm (3/4 in) wide and 1 cm (1/2 in) high.
6 Place the logs, not too close together, on the prepared baking tray. Beat the egg white until it is foamy, and brush it over the logs.
7 Bake the logs in the oven for 20 minutes, until golden brown.
8 Remove the logs from the oven and, with a long serrated knife, cut them into diagonal slices about 5 mm (1/4 in) thick. Reduce the oven temperature to 140°C (275°F, Gas 1), and bake the slices for 30–40 minutes until dry, hard, and lightly browned. Let cool.

VARIATIONS

GINGER BISCOTTI: Add *2 tsp ground ginger* to the eggs and sugar before blending them together.
BISCOTTI WITH RAISINS: Substitute *raisins* for half of the almonds. Add to the dough with the almonds.
HONEY BISCOTTI: Substitute *125 ml (4 fl oz) mild-flavoured honey, such as clover or acacia,* for the sugars, and add up to *90 g (3 oz) extra flour.*

CHOCOLATE CHIP COOKIES

Makes about 80

INGREDIENTS

150 g (5 oz) plain flour
1/2 tsp bicarbonate of soda
1/2 tsp salt
90 g (3 oz) unsalted butter, softened
60 g (2 oz) caster sugar
60 g (2 oz) light soft brown sugar
1 egg, beaten
1/2 tsp vanilla extract
150 g (5 oz) chocolate chips

PREPARATION

1 Sift together the flour, bicarbonate of soda, and salt. Beat together the butter and sugars. Beat the egg and vanilla extract into the butter mixture. Gradually beat in the flour mixture. Stir in the chocolate chips.

2 Divide the dough in half and wrap each piece in wax paper. Chill in the refrigerator for 1 hour, or place in the freezer for 20 minutes, until firm.

3 Flour your hands and shape the dough into logs 2.5 cm (1 in) in diameter. Wrap in lightly floured wax paper and chill in the refrigerator for 1 hour.

4 Remove the logs from the refrigerator one at a time, and cut into 5-mm (1/4-in) slices. Place on ungreased baking trays and bake in a preheated 190°C (375° F, Gas 5) oven for about 8 minutes, until golden brown. Let stand for a few minutes. Transfer to racks and let cool.

 Make batches of dough well in advance and freeze or chill them until ready to bake.

LEMON SABLES

Sablé dough is great for making into different shapes for special occasions. For Christmas, it can be cut into stars, angels, or Christmas trees, while for Valentine's Day it can be cut into hearts.
Makes about 36

INGREDIENTS

175 g (6 oz) unsalted butter, more for greasing
175 g (6 oz) caster sugar
1 egg, beaten
2 tbsp finely chopped lemon zest
2 tbsp lemon juice
300 g (10 oz) plain flour
1 tsp baking powder
1/2 tsp salt

PREPARATION

1 Mix the butter and sugar together in an electric mixer, or in a food processor fitted with the metal blade. Beat in the egg, lemon zest, and lemon juice.

2 Sift together the flour, baking powder, and salt. Add to the butter mixture and combine well. Gather the dough together into a ball, and place in the refrigerator overnight or in the freezer for 1–2 hours.

3 Butter 2–3 baking trays. Cut the dough into quarters and roll out each quarter on to a lightly floured work surface. Cut into small shapes and place on the prepared baking trays.

4 Bake in a preheated 180°C (350°F, Gas 4) oven for 10 minutes, until lightly browned. Transfer to racks and let cool.

COCONUT TUILES

Makes about 25

INGREDIENTS

90 g (3 oz) butter, softened, more for greasing
125 g (4 oz) icing sugar, sifted
3 egg whites
90 g (3 oz) plain flour, sifted
2 tsp double cream
2 tbsp freshly grated or desiccated coconut

PREPARATION

1 Beat the butter with the icing sugar in a bowl until it is pale and creamy. Add about half of the egg whites to the butter mixture, and beat well.

2 Gradually stir in the flour, remaining egg whites, and the cream. Beat until the mixture is smooth.

3 Grease a baking tray with butter and, for each tuile, put 1 tbsp of the mixture on to the tray, spacing each well apart. Sprinkle the freshly grated or desiccated coconut over the edges of the tuiles.

4 Bake in a preheated oven at 200°C (400°F, Gas 6) for about 5 minutes, or until the tuiles are a delicate golden colour.

5 Remove from the oven and immediately slide a palette knife under the tuiles to prevent them from sticking. Quickly curve the tuiles on a greased rolling pin, coconut-side up, and let stand on their edges until set.

A Summer Party

Fresh flavours and crisp textures complement the heat of summer.
Barbecued kebabs are ideal for an outdoor party and
fresh fruit and vegetables are a must.

Vegetable crudités
and Creamy
Curried Dip (page 29)

Choux Puffs (page 138)
with Goat's Cheese
& Pepper filling
(page 50)

Tuna & Red Pepper Kebabs (page 99)
Prawn & Pepper Kebabs (page 98)

Cherry Tomato Cups
(page 148) stuffed with Basil
Pesto (page 25)

Fresh Fruit Tartlets
(page 114)

SPONGE CAKES & MERINGUES

Sponges are quick and economical to make. Cut them into a variety of shapes with a pastry cutter, and layer or top them with creamy fillings. Meringues and macaroons are ideal when serving large numbers, because they can be made weeks in advance. Decorate them with brightly coloured fruit, icings, and fillings for an eye-catching presentation.

★

CHOCOLATE FANCIES

In this recipe, Sponge Cake is layered and then cut into small squares to make delicious little cakes.
Makes 16

INGREDIENTS

20-cm (8-in) square Sponge Cake (see page 152)
200 g (7 oz) white chocolate, broken into small pieces
FOR THE VANILLA BUTTERCREAM FILLING
250 g (8 oz) icing sugar, sifted
45 g (1 1/2 oz) butter, softened
1 1/2 tbsp milk
1 tsp vanilla extract (see page 156)

PREPARATION

1 Cut the cake horizontally into 2 layers.
2 Make the vanilla buttercream filling: mix the ingredients together with an electric mixer, until smooth and fluffy.
3 Using a palette knife, spread the buttercream over 1 layer of cake. Place the second sponge layer on top and chill in the refrigerator for 5 minutes.
4 Melt the chocolate as directed on page 150.
5 Cut the cake into 16 x 5-cm (2-in) squares with a knife that has been dipped in hot water and dried. Make sure that the edges are neat.
6 Set a wire rack over a baking tray. Place the cakes on the rack, then pour the melted chocolate over to cover them evenly. Let the excess chocolate drip on to the baking tray (it can be scraped off and re-used if required). Let stand until the chocolate has set.
7 Put the remaining buttercream into a paper piping bag (see page 151), and pipe a decoration on top of each cake.

VARIATION

MINI FRUIT SANDWICHES: Spread a layer of *fruit jam* over the cake before the buttercream filling. Cut the chilled layered cake into 16 rounds with a 5-cm (2-in) pastry cutter. Decorate with *fresh fruit* and *whipped cream*.

CHOCOLATE MERINGUES

Makes 18

INGREDIENTS

4 egg whites
250 g (8 oz) caster sugar
125 g (4 oz) plain chocolate, broken into small pieces, for the topping
FOR THE GANACHE FILLING
125 g (4 oz) plain chocolate, broken into small pieces
125 ml (4 fl oz) double cream

PREPARATION

1 Whisk the egg whites using an electric whisk, until soft peaks form. Add the caster sugar, 1 tbsp at a time, and continue whisking until it is fully incorporated and the mixture is stiff and shiny.
2 Put the meringue mixture into a piping bag fitted with a small star nozzle. Pipe the mixture into 36 x 5-cm (2-in) rosettes on baking trays lined with parchment paper.
3 Bake the meringues in a preheated oven at 120°C (250°F, Gas 1/2) for 1 hour, or until the meringues are firm and can be easily lifted off the paper. Turn off the oven and leave the meringues in the oven until cold.
4 Make the ganache filling: put the chocolate pieces into a bowl. Pour the cream into a saucepan and bring just to a boil. Pour the hot cream over the chocolate pieces and stir until the chocolate has melted. Whisk the mixture with an electric whisk for about 5 minutes, until the ganache mixture is fluffy and has cooled.
5 Melt the chocolate for the topping as directed on page 150.
6 Drizzle the melted chocolate from a fork over the tops of the meringues, then let stand for 5–10 minutes, until the chocolate has set.
7 Sandwich the meringues together in pairs with the ganache filling.

FRUIT MERINGUES

The combination of whisked egg whites, whipped cream, and fresh fruit is irresistible – as in these "mini Pavlovas", which are illustrated below.
Makes 35

INGREDIENTS

4 egg whites
250 g (8 oz) caster sugar
250 ml (8 fl oz) double cream
2 tbsp lemon curd (optional)
fresh fruit, such as strawberries, blueberries, raspberries, oranges, and kiwi fruit
sprigs of mint for decoration (optional)

PREPARATION

1 Whisk the egg whites using an electric whisk, until soft peaks form. Add the caster sugar, 1 tbsp at a time, and continue whisking until it is fully incorporated and the mixture is stiff and shiny.
2 Put the meringue mixture into a piping bag fitted with a small 1-cm (1/2-in) nozzle. Pipe the mixture into 35 x 5-cm (2-in) rounds on baking trays lined with parchment paper.
3 Bake the meringues in a preheated oven at 120°C (250°F, Gas 1/2) for 1 hour, or until the meringues are firm and can be easily lifted off the paper. Turn off the oven and leave the meringues in the oven until cold.
4 Whip the cream until it forms stiff peaks, then fold in the lemon curd if using. Spoon a little cream on to each meringue round, top with fresh fruit, and decorate with mint sprigs if using.

COFFEE MACAROONS

Macaroons, originally from Venice, have been made for centuries. In this recipe, they are sandwiched together with a buttercream filling.
Makes about 45

INGREDIENTS

250 g (8 oz) icing sugar
200 g (7 oz) ground almonds
3 egg whites
1 tbsp caster sugar
2 tsp instant coffee granules dissolved in
1 tbsp boiling water
FOR THE COFFEE BUTTERCREAM FILLING
125 g (4 oz) icing sugar, sifted
125 g (4 oz) butter
2 tsp instant coffee granules dissolved in
1 tbsp boiling water

PREPARATION

1 Sift the icing sugar and ground almonds together.
2 Whisk the egg whites and caster sugar with a metal whisk or an electric mixer until stiff and shiny. Stir in the dissolved coffee granules.
3 Cut and fold the icing sugar and almond mixture into the egg white mixture with a metal spoon.
4 Put the macaroon mixture into a piping bag fitted with a 1-cm (1/2-in) nozzle. Pipe the mixture into about 90 x 2.5-cm (1-in) rounds on baking trays lined with parchment paper.
5 Bake in a preheated oven at 200°C (400°F, Gas 6) for about 12 minutes or until a light crust forms. Let cool slightly, then peel the macaroons off the paper. Transfer the macaroons to a wire rack and let cool completely.
6 Make the buttercream filling: beat the icing sugar and the butter together with an electric mixer for 10 minutes, or until fluffy. Gradually beat in the dissolved coffee until well combined.
7 Sandwich the macaroons together in pairs with the coffee buttercream filling.

Orange & Kiwi Fruit Meringues

Strawberry Meringues

Blueberry Meringues

FRESH FRUIT PLATTERS

Colourful and refreshing, fruit platters should have a prominent place on a party table. The fruit can be served *au nature*, or with a selection of creamy dips. Choose fruits that are easy to handle – they shouldn't drip – and have plenty of cocktail sticks on hand for spearing them.

SUMMER FRUIT PLATTER

Serves 12

INGREDIENTS

1 ripe honeydew melon
500-g (1-lb) piece of watermelon
1 ripe pineapple
500 g (1 lb) ripe strawberries, with hulls
500 g (1 lb) apricots
500 g (1 lb) ripe but firm peaches
500 g (1 lb) ripe but firm nectarines
500 g (1 lb) fresh figs
500 g (1 lb) cherries, with stalks
Creamy Dips of your choice (see page 134)

PREPARATION

1 Using a melon baller, scoop out balls from the flesh of both the melons.
2 Peel the pineapple and quarter it lengthways. Cut out the core from each piece, then cut the pineapple into bite-sized pieces.
3 Halve the strawberries lengthways. Halve and stone the apricots. Halve, stone, and slice the peaches and nectarines. Quarter the figs.
4 Distribute the fruits over platters and serve the dips in individual bowls.

VARIATIONS

MEXICAN FRUIT PLATTER (see page 101): Combine *500 g (1 lb) watermelon chunks* with *4 mangoes, peeled, stoned, and sliced; 6 passion fruit, halved;* and *2 star fruit, sliced crossways.* Spear *500 g (1 lb) pineapple chunks* on cocktail sticks, dip in *melted chocolate,* and use to fill *6 large papaya halves.*
ORIENTAL FRUIT PLATTER (see pages 86–87): Combine *500 g (1 lb) fresh lychees, peeled,* with *2 papayas, peeled, seeded, and cut into 1-cm (1/2-in) dice; 12 mandarins, peeled and segmented; 2 prickly pears, quartered lengthways; 2 large Asian pears, cut into chevrons; 2 star fruit, sliced crossways; 6 passion fruit, halved; 2 pomegranates, quartered lengthways;* and *12 kumquats, halved lengthways.*

Orange & Cointreau Dip

Pistachio Dip

Chocolate Dip

Ginger Dip

133

CREAMY DIPS

Whipped cream sweetened with a little sugar is the simplest of dips to serve with fresh fruit. Crème Anglaise can also be served as a dip. It takes a little more time and trouble than simply whipping cream, but it does add a touch of luxury to a platter of fresh fruit. Serve it plain (see page 153) or flavour it, as in the recipes here. All these dips will keep for 1 day in the refrigerator.

★

ORANGE & COINTREAU DIP

Makes about 300 ml (1/2 pint)

INGREDIENTS

2 tbsp whipping cream
2 tbsp Cointreau or other orange-flavoured liqueur
finely grated zest of 1 orange
250 ml (8 fl oz) Crème Anglaise (see page 153), cooled

PREPARATION

1 Whip the cream until it just holds its shape.
2 Stir the Cointreau and grated orange zest into the Crème Anglaise, then fold in the cream until evenly incorporated.

CHOCOLATE DIP

Makes about 300 ml (1/2 pint)

INGREDIENTS

90 g (3 oz) plain chocolate, broken into small pieces
250 ml (8 fl oz) Crème Anglaise (see page 153)
2 tbsp whipping cream

PREPARATION

1 Put the chocolate pieces in a bowl placed over a saucepan of gently simmering water and heat gently until melted. Remove the bowl from the pan and let the chocolate cool for 5 minutes.
2 Stir the melted chocolate into the Crème Anglaise until evenly blended. Let cool.
3 Whip the cream until it just holds its shape. Fold into the Crème Anglaise mixture until evenly incorporated.

GINGER DIP

Makes about 300 ml (1/2 pint)

INGREDIENTS

1/4 – 1/2 tsp ground ginger
1/4 tsp vanilla extract (see page 156)
250 ml (8 fl oz) Crème Anglaise (see page 153), cooled
2 tbsp whipping cream

PREPARATION

1 Stir the ground ginger and vanilla extract into the Crème Anglaise until evenly mixed.
2 Whip the cream until it just holds its shape. Fold the cream into the Crème Anglaise mixture until evenly incorporated.

PISTACHIO DIP

Makes about 300 ml (1/2 pint)

INGREDIENTS

60 g (2 oz) shelled and skinned pistachios
250 ml (8 fl oz) Crème Anglaise (see page 153), cooled
2 tbsp whipping cream
green food colouring (optional)

PREPARATION

1 Work the pistachios in a food processor fitted with the metal blade until very finely ground. Press through a sieve with a metal spoon into the Crème Anglaise. Beat well to mix.
2 Whip the cream until it just holds its shape.
3 Fold the cream into the Crème Anglaise mixture until evenly incorporated, adding a drop or two of food colouring, if you prefer.

TECHNIQUES

*Here are the basic techniques and recipes on which
many of the finger foods and appetizers in this book
are based. You will find inspirational ideas for simple
vegetable containers and beautiful garnishes.
Instructions are given to help you prepare pastries for
quiches, tartlets, choux puffs, and gougères, and
doughs for pizza and focaccia. Recipes and
instructions are included for blini, crêpes, and
filo shapes, as well as for sponge cakes. Clever ways
with chocolate are also explained. Step-by-step
illustrations make each recipe easy to follow.*

PASTRIES

The main ingredient of pastry is flour. Fat, eggs, and water are added in varying proportions for flavour, colour, and texture. Use Pâte Brisée or Yeasted Olive Oil Pastry for quiches, and Pâte Sucrée or rich and crumbly Rough Puff Pastry for sweet tartlets. Fill choux puffs with cream, or add cheese to the dough for gougères.

★

PATE BRISEE

You can make Pâte Brisée from plain white flour or wholewheat flour. Wholewheat pastry will have a much nuttier flavour than Pâte Brisée, but it is a little trickier to roll out because it tends to crumble.
Enough for 8–10 x 7-cm (3-in) quiche shells

INGREDIENTS

175 g (6 oz) plain white flour,
or 175 g (6 oz) wholewheat flour,
or 90 g (3 oz) wholewheat flour
and 90 g (3 oz) plain white flour
¹/4 tsp salt
90 g (3 oz) cold butter, cut into small pieces
2–3 tbsp ice-cold water

1 Combine the flour and salt in a large bowl. Quickly cut in the butter and roll briskly between the palms of your hands to make sure that the butter is evenly distributed. The mixture should have the consistency of crumbs.

2 Add water to the dry mixture 1 tbsp at a time, and blend with a fork until the dough comes together. Shape the dough into a ball. Refrigerate for 20 minutes or longer.

3 When ready to use the dough, place the ball on a lightly floured work surface, and press it down gently with your fingertips so that it is about 2.5 cm (1 in) thick.

ROLLING OUT DOUGH & LINING QUICHE TINS

To roll out dough, lightly dust the rolling pin and work surface with flour to prevent sticking. A cool surface, such as marble, is especially good. Roll out the dough in one direction only, without stretching it, otherwise it will shrink during baking. Handle the dough as little as possible: if it becomes elastic, it will be difficult to roll out.

Roll out wholewheat dough between parchment paper to prevent cracking.

1 Roll out the dough into a 30-cm (12-in) round. Cut rounds with appropriate pastry cutters, depending on the size of the finished tartlets.

2 Line tins with dough rounds, and gently press into the edges of the tins. Refrigerate, covered, for 2 hours to relax the pastry.

YEASTED OLIVE OIL PASTRY

This dough is very light compared to a butter dough, and is extremely easy to work with.
Enough for 8–10 x 7-cm (3-in) quiche shells

INGREDIENTS

4 tbsp lukewarm water
1 tsp dried yeast
150 g (5 oz) wholewheat flour
150 g (5 oz) plain flour
1/2–3/4 tsp salt
1 large egg
4 tbsp olive oil

Making Pastry Dough in a Machine

For Pâte Brisée, *place the flour or flours and salt in a food processor fitted with the metal blade. Pulse a few times to combine the ingredients. Add the butter in small pieces and pulse on and off about 30 times, until the mixture resembles crumbs. With the machine running, add the water, 1 tbsp at a time. As soon as the dough comes together, remove from the food processor and shape into a ball.*

For Yeasted Olive Oil Pastry, *follow step 1 of the recipe, then, using the paddle, combine all the ingredients in the bowl of an electric mixer. Switch to the dough hook and continue mixing until the dough comes together; remove, and shape into a ball.*

1 Put the lukewarm water in a small bowl, sprinkle over the yeast, and let stand for 5–10 minutes, until the yeast dissolves to a smooth paste.

2 In a large bowl, combine the flours with salt to taste, and stir in the yeast mixture. Beat in the egg and olive oil. Work into a dough, and knead a few minutes, then shape into a ball.

3 Place in a lightly oiled bowl, cover, and let rise in a warm place for 2 hours. The dough will not rise much, but it will expand and soften. Remove and punch it down gently. Cover, and let rest for 10 minutes.

PRESSING DOUGH INTO QUICHE TINS

Instead of being rolled out, pastry dough can be pressed directly into tins. This method is particularly useful for wholewheat pastry dough, which can break when being rolled out. Divide the dough into the same number of portions as quiche tins, form into balls, and pat out into rounds to fit the tins. For a large quiche, press the dough out towards the side with the heel of your hand. For smaller quiches, use your fingertips.

1 Divide the dough into pieces. Shape into balls and press them flat between the palms of your hands. Place a round of dough in each tin.

2 Using your fingertips, spread the dough out from the centre of the tin towards the side. Cover loosely and let rest for 20–30 minutes.

CHOUX PASTRY

Enough for 40 x 3.5-cm (1¹/2-in) choux puffs or gougères

INGREDIENTS

250 ml (8 fl oz) water
90 g (3 oz) unsalted butter
1 tsp caster sugar
salt
150 g (5 oz) plain flour, sifted
4 large eggs

FOR GOUGERES

60 g (2 oz) Gruyère cheese, grated

MAKING PERFECT CHOUX PASTRY

- *The flour must be added all at once to the butter and water mixture. This will be easier if you sift the flour on to a large piece of paper, which you can then use as a funnel when adding the flour.*

- *Make sure the mixture comes away from the pan before you add the eggs.*

- *You may not need to use up all of the eggs. Stop before the mixture becomes too slack.*

---

1 Put the water, butter, sugar, and a pinch of salt into a 1.5-litre (2¹/2-pint) saucepan and bring to a boil. Reduce the heat slightly and simmer gently until the butter has melted.

2 Remove from the heat and add the flour all at once, stirring vigorously and constantly with a wooden spoon. Return to a medium-high heat and stir until the mixture comes away from the side of the pan in a mass and a film forms on the bottom of the pan.

3 Remove from the heat. Add 1 egg and beat in well. Beat the remaining eggs into the paste 1 at a time, then beat until the mixture is soft and shiny. (For gougères: reserve 2 tbsp cheese for topping, and beat in ¹/4 of the remainder with each egg.)

PIPING & BAKING CHOUX PASTRY

1 Fill a piping bag fitted with a 3.5-cm (1¹/2-in) star nozzle with choux paste. On buttered baking trays, pipe 7-cm (3-in) lengths for gougères, or 3.5-cm (1¹/2-in) mounds for puffs, spaced apart.

2 Brush the tops carefully with beaten egg. Bake in the upper and lower thirds of a preheated 220°C (425°F, Gas 7) oven for 20 minutes, until golden brown and doubled in size.

3 Remove the pastries and pierce along one side with a sharp knife. Turn off the oven and return the pastries to the oven for another 10 minutes with the door ajar. Remove and cool on racks.

ROUGH PUFF PASTRY

The method given here is easier and quicker than the classic puff pastry method, but it still has plenty of buttery, feathery layers. Use the pastry to make tart or tartlet shells (see box, below) and fill with fresh fruit, or use for Napoleons, palmiers, or other ornamental pastries.
Enough for 2 x 25-cm (10-in) tarts or 36 small tartlets

INGREDIENTS

300 g (10 oz) unsalted butter, chopped and chilled
300 g (10 oz) plain flour, sifted with ¹/2 tsp salt
5–6 tbsp ice-cold water

1 Divide the butter into 4 equal portions. Rub 1 portion into the flour until evenly distributed. Add the water, 1 tbsp at a time, and blend with a fork until the dough can be gathered up into a ball. Wrap and refrigerate for 30 minutes.

2 Roll out the dough into a rectangle 1 cm (¹/2 in) thick. Scatter ¹/3 of the remaining butter over ²/3 of the dough. Fold over the unbuttered ¹/3, then fold over again to cover the exposed buttered portion that remains.

3 Turn the package over and seal the 2 narrow ends together with a rolling pin. Wrap and refrigerate for 15–30 minutes.

4 Remove from the refrigerator, unwrap, and roll out into a rectangle 1 cm (¹/2 in) thick. Repeat step 2, using ¹/2 of the remaining butter, and then step 3.

5 Remove from the refrigerator, unwrap, and roll out as in step 4. Repeat step 2, using the remaining butter, and then step 3.

6 Remove from the refrigerator, unwrap, and repeat step 2 without butter. Wrap and refrigerate for at least 15–30 minutes, or preferably for longer (2 hours or until ready to use).

MAKING PASTRY SHELLS

Remove the dough from the refrigerator and divide into 2 equal pieces for large tarts or 4 pieces for tartlets. Roll out to 2.5–5-mm (¹/8–¹/4-in) thickness. For tartlets, cut out 36 rounds. Line tart or tartlet tins (prick the pastry for large tarts) and refrigerate for 15–30 minutes. Brush with egg glaze, and bake in a preheated 200°C (400°F, Gas 6) oven for 10 minutes, then at 180°C (350°F, Gas 4) for another 10–20 minutes.

PATE SUCREE

*This is a sweet pastry for dessert tarts or tartlets.
Enough for 1 x 25- x 30-cm (10- x 12-in) or 1 x 25-cm
(10-in) tart shell, or 24 x 5-cm (2-in) or 16 x 7-cm (3-in)
tartlet shells*

INGREDIENTS

*175 g (6 oz) plain flour, sifted
1—2 tbsp caster sugar (use the larger amount
if you prefer a sweeter pastry)
¹/4 tsp salt
90 g (3 oz) unsalted butter
2—3 tbsp ice-cold water*

PREPARATION

1 Place the flour, sugar, and salt in a large bowl and
combine well.
2 Quickly cut the butter into the mixture and
roll the mixture briskly between the palms of
your hands to make sure the butter is evenly
distributed. The mixture should have the
consistency of crumbs.
3 Add the water, 1 tbsp at a time, and blend with a
fork until the dough forms a ball.
4 Place the dough on a sheet of lightly floured
parchment paper. Press it down so that it is
about 2.5 cm (1 in) thick and cover with another
sheet of lightly floured parchment paper.
Refrigerate the dough for 20 minutes or longer
before rolling out.

MAKING PASTRY DOUGH IN
A FOOD PROCESSOR

*Place the dry ingredients in the bowl of a food processor
fitted with the metal blade. Pulse a few times. Cut the
butter into small pieces and add to the bowl. Pulse on and
off about 30 times, until the mixture resembles crumbs.
With the machine running, add the almond extract, if
using in the Almond Dessert Pastry, and the water, 1 tbsp
at a time. As soon as the dough comes together, stop the
machine and remove the dough. Shape into a ball.*

ALMOND DESSERT PASTRY

*This dessert pastry has a rich, nutty flavour. I use it more
often than Pâte Sucrée, especially for fruit tarts. It is
slightly more difficult to roll out, so place a piece of
parchment paper over the dough when you roll it.
Enough for 1 x 25-cm (10-in) tart shell,
16 x 5-cm (2-in) or 10 x 7-cm (3-in) tartlet shells*

INGREDIENTS

*60 g (2 oz) ground almonds
125 g (4 oz) plain flour, sifted
2 tbsp caster sugar
¹/4 tsp salt
90 g (3 oz) unsalted butter
1 drop of almond extract (optional) see page 156
2—3 tbsp ice-cold water*

PREPARATION

1 Place the ground almonds, flour, sugar, and salt
in a large bowl and combine well.
2 Quickly cut the butter into the mixture and roll
the mixture briskly between the palms of your
hands to make sure the butter is evenly
distributed. The mixture should have the
consistency of crumbs.
3 Add the almond extract if using, and the water,
1 tbsp at a time, and blend in with a fork until
you can gather the dough into a ball.
4 Place the dough on a sheet of lightly floured
parchment paper. Press it down so that it is about
2.5 cm (1 in) thick and cover with another sheet
of lightly floured parchment paper. Refrigerate
for 1 hour or longer before rolling out.

*Both Pâte Sucrée and Almond Dessert Pastry can
be chilled in the refrigerator for up to 4 days.
They can also be frozen, before rolling out or
after making tart or tartlet shells, for 3 months.
Transfer frozen pastry shells directly from the
freezer to the oven for prebaking.*

LINING TARTLET TINS WITH SWEET PASTRY

Pâte Sucrée and Almond Dessert Pastry are quite crumbly because of the sugar and ground nut content, so they can be difficult to roll out. Your work surface should be cold – marble is ideal, but ceramic and granite are also good.

Remove the dough from the refrigerator. If the dough is too firm to roll easily, knock it with the rolling pin to make it more pliable. Dust the work surface and rolling pin lightly with flour. Place a sheet of parchment paper over the dough to prevent it from cracking, and roll out in one direction only, to 5-mm (¼-in) thickness. Do not stretch the dough, because this will cause shrinkage during baking.

1 Cut out rounds using an appropriate pastry cutter, depending on the size of the finished tartlets. Use a firm downward action, without twisting, to prevent stretching the dough. Ease each round gently off the work surface with a palette knife and place in a tin.

2 Gently press the rounds into the edges of the tins. Run a rolling pin over the edge of each tin and trim off the extra pastry. Prick the bottoms of the shells in several places. Refrigerate, covered, for 2 hours or double wrap and freeze for up to 3 months.

MAKING A LARGE RECTANGULAR TART SHELL

One large tart is much easier to make, fill, and bake than a number of small tartlets, and it can easily be cut into bite-sized pieces.

However, you may find a large piece of dough difficult to roll out. To make it more manageable, make sure the dough is well chilled and handle it as little as possible.

Dust the work surface and rolling pin lightly with flour. Place a sheet of parchment paper over the dough to prevent it from cracking, and roll out in one direction only, to 5-mm (¼-in) thickness. Do not stretch the dough, because this will cause shrinkage during baking.

1 Lift the dough on to a rolling pin and unroll it on to a lightly greased 30-x 25-cm (12-x 10-in) baking tin.

2 Fit the dough into the corners and up the sides of the tin, smoothing out wrinkles with a small ball of dough.

BAKING TART & TARTLET SHELLS

To bake tart and tartlet shells blind: line the shells loosely with foil, shiny-side up. Push the foil into the corners to prevent the pastry from shrinking. Weight the foil down with baking beans or rice.

For a partially baked shell, bake 25-cm (10-in) tart shells in a preheated 190°C (375°F, Gas 5) oven for 20 minutes, and 5–7-cm (2–3-in) tartlet shells for 10 minutes, until the edges are lightly browned. Remove the foil and beans and bake for a further 10 minutes for

a tart shell, or 5 minutes for tartlet shells, until the crust is golden.

For fully baked shells: bake tart shells for a further 20 minutes, or tartlet shells for a further 10 minutes, until browned. Remove from the heat and let cool for 5–10 minutes, until you can handle the shells without breaking them, then remove the shells from the tins.

FILO SHAPES

Paper-thin filo pastry can be wrapped around delicious savoury fillings (see pages 76–77) in a variety of shapes: classic *tiropites* or triangles, money bags with scrunched tops, tubular cigars, or little square parcels tied up with a pretty garnish.

Brush with melted butter and olive oil at all stages and especially the finished pastry. Keep pastry you are not working with wrapped in a damp tea towel. Filo pastry is available ready-made, but if you have trouble finding it, you could make it yourself (see page 143).

★

TIROPITES (TRIANGLES)

1 With a sharp knife, cut 6-cm (2¹/2-in) wide strips from the length of each sheet of filo pastry. Brush each strip with a mixture of melted butter and olive oil.

2 Place 1 tsp of the chosen filling at one end of a strip. Lifting a corner, fold the pastry diagonally over the filling until the shorter edge of the strip meets the longer edge.

3 Continue folding over and over, alternately at right angles then diagonally, until you reach the end of the strip. Seal and brush with more melted butter and olive oil mixture.

MONEY BAGS

1 With a sharp knife, cut 6-cm (2¹/2-in) wide strips from the length of each sheet of filo pastry. Cut each strip into 6-cm (2¹/2-in) squares.

2 Brush a square of pastry with a mixture of melted butter and olive oil and place another square on top at an angle. Grease again and repeat with a third square to form a 12-pointed star.

3 Place 1 tsp of the chosen filling in the centre of the pastry and bring all the corners together around it. Twist to secure, and brush with more melted butter and olive oil mixture.

CIGARS

1 With a sharp knife, cut 6-cm (2¹/2-in) wide strips from each sheet of filo pastry. Brush the long edges with a mixture of melted butter and olive oil.

2 Place 1 tsp of the filling, centred, near one end of a strip. Fold the long edges over the filling and along the length of the strip.

3 Fold the short end over the filling and continue rolling up the strip until you reach the end. Seal and brush the cigars with the melted butter and oil.

PARCELS

1 Brush a 6-cm (2¹/2-in) square of filo pastry with melted butter and olive oil. Place 1 tsp filling in the centre and fold over one of the edges.

2 Fold the opposite edge over the filling to overlap the first edge. Brush with melted butter and olive oil. Fold over a third edge and brush again.

3 Fold the final edge over in the opposite direction, so that the filling is covered with equal layers of pastry on either side. Brush again.

MAKING FILO PASTRY BY HAND

Enough for about 60 pastries

INGREDIENTS

250 g (8 oz) plain flour, more for dusting
1 egg, beaten
2 tbsp sunflower or rapeseed oil
4 tbsp warm water

PREPARATION

1 Sift the flour and a pinch of salt into a bowl. Add the egg, oil, and water. Mix to a soft, sticky dough.

2 Turn the dough on to a floured surface and knead for 5–7 minutes, until smooth and shiny. Cover with a bowl and let stand for 30 minutes.

3 Lightly flour the work surface and the dough, and roll out the dough into a large square. Cover with a damp tea towel and let stand for 15 minutes. Place floured hands under the dough and stretch it out from the centre until it is about 1 metre (1 yard) square.

BASIC PIZZA & FOCACCIA

Pizza and focaccia doughs are both made with yeast. They require kneading, to build up the gluten content that binds the dough, and they need to rest in a warm place, so that the yeast can work on the dough to make it rise.

★

MAKING A PIZZA BASE

This dough is very easy to handle. Use it to make large or medium pizzas, small pizzettas, or calzone (see pages 63–67). The rolled-out dough can be baked either in pizza pans or directly on a baking stone (see page 156).
Makes 2 large pizzas, 3 medium pizzas, 16–20 pizzettas, or 36 calzone

INGREDIENTS

2 tsp dried yeast
350 ml (12 fl oz) lukewarm water
625 g (1 1/4 lb) plain flour,
plus 60 g (2 oz) plain flour for kneading
2 tsp salt

1 Dissolve the yeast in 4 tbsp of the lukewarm water, and let stand for 5 minutes, until the yeast begins to bubble. Mix in the remaining water.

2 Mix 125 g (4 oz) flour with the salt, and stir in. Fold in the remaining flour, about 60 g (2 oz) at a time, until the dough holds its shape.

3 Knead the dough on a floured surface for 10 minutes, adding flour as necessary, until the dough becomes very elastic. Shape into a ball.

4 Place the dough in a bowl lightly oiled with olive oil, and roll it around in the bowl to coat with the oil. Cover with a tea towel, and leave to rise in a warm place for 1 1/2–2 hours, or until the dough doubles in volume.

5 Punch down the dough and divide it into the number of pieces required (see above). Roll out each piece no thicker than 5 mm (1/4 in). Keep the other pieces covered with a damp tea towel.

6 Oil baking trays or pizza pans, and sprinkle with cornmeal (polenta) or semolina. For pizzas and pizzettas, roll the edges of the dough in and pinch a lip all the way round.

MAKING FOCACCIA

Focaccia dough is more moist than pizza dough, and therefore slightly more unwieldy. The finished breads should be about 2.5 cm (1 in) thick, and soft. Makes 2 x 26- x 38-cm (10¹/2- x 15¹/2-in) rectangular focaccias

INGREDIENTS

2 tsp dried yeast
500 ml (16 fl oz) lukewarm water
4 tbsp olive oil
650–750 g (1¹/3–1¹/2 lb) plain flour,
or 375 g (12 oz) plain flour and 375 g (12 oz)
wholewheat flour, plus additional plain flour for kneading
2¹/2 tsp salt
1 tbsp olive oil for brushing the tops

1 Dissolve the yeast in the water, and let stand for 10 minutes. Stir in the olive oil.

2 Combine the flour and salt, and fold in all but 150 g (5 oz) of it, until the dough holds its shape.

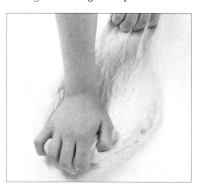

3 Knead on a lightly floured surface for 10 minutes, adding flour until the dough is elastic. Shape into a ball.

4 Roll in a bowl lightly oiled with olive oil. Cover with a damp tea towel, and let rise in a warm place for 1¹/2–2 hours, or until doubled in size.

5 Turn out on to a lightly floured work surface, knead for 1 minute, then cut into 2 pieces. Shape into 2 balls.

6 Oil 2 baking trays and dust with cornmeal (polenta). Roll or press out the dough to just about fit the trays. Cover, and let rest for 10 minutes.

7 Press the dough out to the edges of the baking trays. Cover with damp tea towels, and let rise for 1 hour, until the dough is puffed up.

8 Dimple the tops all over, and brush lightly with olive oil. Bake in a preheated 200°C (400°F, Gas 6) oven, preferably with a baking stone in it (see page 156), for 20–25 minutes, until the tops are golden brown. Cool on racks.

MAKING PIZZA & FOCACCIA IN AN ELECTRIC MIXER

Dissolve the yeast in the mixer bowl; let stand for 10 minutes. Stir in the oil. If making focaccia, reserve 90 g (3 oz) of the flour. Mix the flour and salt into the yeast mixture with the mixing attachment. Knead for 2 minutes with the dough hook at low speed, then for 10 minutes at medium speed, adding more flour for focaccia. Knead for 1 minute by hand and shape into a ball. Continue from step 4.

BLINI & CREPES

These are both made from egg and milk batters. Blini batter has yeast added to it, which makes the blini thick and spongy. Crêpe batter is thinner, and spread around the pan so that the finished crêpe can be wrapped around a filling.

★

BLINI

You can make blini from buckwheat or fine cornmeal (polenta). Buckwheat blini will be darker than cornmeal – they are excellent for fish toppings. Cornmeal blini are grainy in texture, and well suited to Mexican-style toppings. A heavy griddle is best for cooking blini, but you can also cook them in a crêpe pan or a non-stick frying pan.
Makes 50 x 5-cm (2-in) blini

INGREDIENTS

1 tsp dried yeast
2 tbsp lukewarm water
275 ml (9 fl oz) plus 2 tbsp lukewarm low-fat milk
125 g (4 oz) stoneground cornmeal or buckwheat flour
125 g (4 oz) plain flour
3/4–1 tsp salt
125 ml (4 fl oz) buttermilk or plain low-fat yogurt
2 large eggs, separated
2 tbsp unsalted butter, melted

1 Dissolve the yeast in the water in a bowl. Stir in the milk and let stand for 5 minutes. Combine the cornmeal or buckwheat flour and the plain flour with salt to taste, and gradually add to the milk. Mix together well. Stir in the buttermilk or yogurt.

2 Beat the egg yolks into the batter. Cover, and let stand in a warm place for 1 hour or until the batter is quite bubbly and spongy.

3 Beat the egg whites to soft peaks and gently fold into the batter. Cover again, and let rise for 1 hour. The batter should be spongy and light.

4 Lightly grease a pan with the melted butter and heat over medium heat. Pour in 1–2 tbsp batter for each blini.

5 Cook for about 1 minute, until bubbles break through. Using a metal spatula, turn the blini over and brown on the other side for 30 seconds.

6 Overlap the blini on a plate as you transfer them from the pan. If they are stacked directly on top of each other, they will become soggy.

CREPES

This recipe is for making batter in a food processor, but you can also make the batter by hand. Sift together the flour and salt. Beat the eggs and stir in the flour and salt mixture, then beat in the milk, water, and butter. Strain through a sieve.
Makes 12–14 crêpes

INGREDIENTS

2 large eggs
175 ml (6 fl oz) milk
125 ml (4 fl oz) water
3 tbsp unsalted butter, melted
$1/2$ tsp salt
125 g (4 oz) plain flour
unsalted butter for the crêpe pan

HERB CREPES
Add 3 tbsp chopped fresh herbs, such as chives, parsley, tarragon, or chervil, to the batter just before making the crêpes.

1 Mix the eggs, milk, water, melted butter, and salt in a food processor or blender, and slowly add the flour with the machine running. Mix at high speed for 1 minute. Refrigerate the batter for 1–2 hours, so that the flour particles can soften and swell.

2 Heat a crêpe pan over medium heat and brush the bottom with butter. When the butter just begins to smoke, remove the pan from the heat, and pour in about 3 tbsp batter. Tilt the pan to distribute the batter evenly.

3 Return the pan to the heat and cook the crêpe for about 1 minute. Loosen the edge gently with a spatula.

4 When the crêpe comes away from the pan easily, turn and cook for about 30 seconds on the other side.

MAKING PERFECT CREPES

• *Use a 15–18-cm (6–7-in) non-stick crêpe pan or, preferably, a seasoned pan which you use only for crêpes. Never wash the pan; just wipe clean with paper towels.*

• *While cooking, have the batter ready in a bowl, with a whisk to hand for stirring, because the flour tends to settle and the batter will need to be stirred before making each crêpe. Also have a small ladle to hand, and a plate on which to stack the finished crêpes.*

• *To prevent crêpes from sticking to the pan, make sure the pan is well seasoned and your batter is well blended so the flour does not settle.*

• *Do not panic if the first few crêpes stick. It might take that many to get the pan saturated with butter.*

• *After the first 3–4 crêpes, you will not need to brush the pan with butter every time.*

• *Turn the crêpe from the pan on to a plate, with the first (or "good") side down.*

PREPARING VEGETABLES

A whole variety of vegetables can be stuffed with delicious fillings, cut into dippers to dunk into savoury dips, or used for garnishing party platters.

Baby vegetables make the daintiest containers and are therefore ideal for finger food. As well as the ideas illustrated here, there are more featured on page 25.

★

COURGETTE BOATS

1 Trim off stalk ends of courgettes and discard. Blanch courgettes in boiling salted water for 1 minute. Drain and rinse under cold water.

2 Using a small sharp knife, cut each courgette in half lengthways.

3 With a sharp-edged teaspoon, carefully scoop out a small amount of flesh from each courgette half.

CUCUMBER CUPS

1 With a fork, score the skin of a cucumber lengthways. Cut the cucumber crossways into 2-cm (3/4-in) slices.

2 Using a melon baller or teaspoon, scoop out the flesh from each slice, leaving a 5-mm (1/4-in) border.

3 Lightly salt the cucumber cups and invert on a rack to drain for about 10 minutes. Rinse before use.

TOMATO CUPS

1 Using a small sharp knife, carefully cut off a thin slice from the stalk ends of cherry tomatoes.

2 With a sharp-edged teaspoon, scoop out the seeds and flesh from the centre of each tomato.

3 Lightly salt inside the hollowed-out tomatoes and invert them on a rack. Let drain briefly and rinse.

CARROT CURLS

1 Cut trimmed and peeled carrots lengthways into 3-mm (¹/8-in) thick strips.

2 Place the carrot strips in a bowl of iced water.

3 Place the bowl of carrot strips in the refrigerator and leave for at least 2–3 hours or overnight, until they become curls.

RADISH ROSES

1 Make a lengthways cut down one side of a radish without slicing right through to the green top.

2 Make 3 more similar cuts around the radish, taking care not to cut off the slices at the top.

3 Place in a bowl of iced water and refrigerate for at least 2–3 hours. The cut sides will curl out to form petals.

SPRING ONION CURLS

1 Trim the roots and most of the green parts from spring onions to form pieces about 6 cm (2¹/2 in) long.

2 Slit the bottoms so they can absorb water. Make several lengthways cuts about 3.5 cm (1¹/2 in) long at the tops.

3 Place in a bowl of iced water and refrigerate for at least 2–3 hours. The fringed tops will curl out.

CHOCOLATE

There are many techniques involving chocolate, none of which are difficult as long as you are patient and careful. Always work in a cool place with cool hands. Melt chocolate gently – the bottom of the bowl should not touch the water in the pan or the chocolate will become overheated and burn. Stir only occasionally during melting. If you overstir, the chocolate will "seize" and stiffen into a hard lump.

MELTING CHOCOLATE

MAKING CHOCOLATE LEAVES

Break chocolate into small pieces, place in a bowl set over a pan of simmering water, and stir with a spoon every 15 seconds until the chocolate melts.

1 Brush melted chocolate on the under-sides of clean, non-toxic leaves with a clean paint brush. Apply a second coat if the first was too thin. Leave to set in the refrigerator for about 30 minutes.

2 With cool hands, carefully peel the leaves away from the chocolate, starting from the stalk end of each leaf.

MAKING CHOCOLATE CUPS

FILLING CHOCOLATE CUPS

1 Brush melted chocolate on the insides of paper or foil petit-four cases. Two layers are usually better than one. Leave the chocolate to set.

2 Make a small tear in the paper case and, with cool hands, carefully peel the case off each chocolate cup.

Put the filling of your choice (see page 125) into a piping bag fitted with a plain or star-shaped nozzle. Pipe the filling neatly into each cup.

MAKING CHOCOLATE CURLS

Hold a bar of chocolate in your hand for a few minutes to warm and soften it slightly. Slowly pass a vegetable peeler over one of the edges to produce softly rounded curls. If the chocolate is hard, it will produce small, coarse shavings.

CHOCOLATE-COATED FRUIT

1 Melt chocolate (see page 150), and remove the pan of water from the heat. Hold each piece of fruit by its stalk, or spear with a cocktail stick, and dip into the melted chocolate until evenly coated.

2 Dip fruit in melted chocolate on one side only or only halfway up. This not only gives a pretty effect, it also lets the fruit stand on its uncoated side so the chocolate dries without smudging.

MAKING & USING A PAPER PIPING BAG

1 Cut out a 20- x 35-cm (8- x 14-in) rectangle of greaseproof paper. Fold over diagonally and cut to form 2 triangles. With the longest edge of 1 triangle facing you, roll the shorter side in to form a cone.

2 Holding the cone firmly with one hand, wrap the longer side over it to reinforce it. Tuck the corner of this side into the cone to secure it. The second triangle can be made into a piping bag in the same way.

3 Fill the cone with 2–3 tbsp melted chocolate or icing and fold over the top of the cone to seal in the filling. Snip the tip of the cone and gently press the chocolate or icing through.

ICING WITH MELTED CHOCOLATE

For a quick and easy decoration, melt chocolate and pipe it from a paper piping bag. Here, melted white chocolate is piped in a free-flow zigzag pattern on Creamy Chocolate & Orange Bouchées (see page 125) set in rectangular chocolate cases.

DESSERT BASICS

These recipes are the basis of many desserts. Cut up Sponge Cake into smaller shapes and top or sandwich with fruit or cream. Plain or flavoured Crème Anglaise makes delicious dips, while thicker Crème Pâtissière is ideal as a filling.

★

SPONGE CAKE

Use this simple cake mixture as a base for petits fours, or small fancies. Butter your cake tin, line with parchment or greaseproof paper, then butter the paper and dust with flour.
Makes 1 x 20-cm (8-in) round or square cake

INGREDIENTS

4 eggs, separated
scant ¹/4 tsp cream of tartar (optional)
150 g (5 oz) caster sugar
1¹/2 tsp vanilla extract (see page 156)
140 g (4¹/2 oz) plain flour
3 tbsp tepid melted butter (optional)

1 Beat the egg whites with a clean, dry whisk, until they begin to foam. Add a pinch of salt and the cream of tartar, if using. Beat until soft peaks form. Add 1¹/2 tbsp of the sugar and beat again until stiff peaks form. Set aside.

2 Beat the egg yolks in another bowl. Beat in the remaining sugar, 1 tbsp at a time, until the mixture is pale yellow and leaves a ribbon trail when the whisk is lifted. Beat in the vanilla. Stir in ¹/4 of the beaten egg whites.

3 Place ¹/3 of the remaining egg whites on top and sift on ¹/4 of the flour. Gently fold in. Repeat with ¹/3 of the remaining egg whites and ¹/4 of the flour; then with ¹/2 of the remaining egg whites and flour.

4 Fold in the remaining egg whites and flour, and then fold in the melted butter, if using.

5 Pour the batter into a prepared round or square cake tin. Tap once against the work surface to deflate large air bubbles. Bake in a preheated 180°C (350°F, Gas 4) oven for 25–30 minutes.

6 Let cool in the tin on a rack for 15–20 minutes. Invert on to another rack, remove the tin, and peel off the lining paper. Invert the cake back on to the first rack and let cool.

CREME ANGLAISE

This is a sweet custard, traditionally used as a sauce to serve with desserts and puddings, but I like to use it as a dip for fresh fruit, either plain or with flavourings added to it (see page 134). It is important to stir the mixture well during cooking, to achieve a smooth consistency. For a truly luxurious custard, stir in a few spoonfuls of cream when cool.
Makes about 500 ml (16 fl oz)

INGREDIENTS

4 large egg yolks
125 g (4 oz) caster sugar
350 ml (12 fl oz) milk
1/2 tsp vanilla extract (see page 156)

1 Beat the egg yolks and sugar together until thick and lemon-coloured. Meanwhile, heat the milk in a heavy-based saucepan to simmering point, then remove from the heat.

2 Beat the milk into the egg-yolk mixture. Pour into a pan and cook over medium-low heat, stirring. Lift the pan off the heat now and then to prevent the eggs from scrambling.

3 Remove from the heat when the custard reaches the consistency of thick cream and coats a spoon evenly. Strain into a bowl and whisk in the vanilla extract. Let cool, then refrigerate.

CREME PATISSIERE

This flour-based egg custard is thick enough to fill choux puffs (see pages 120–121) or to use as a sponge cake filling.
Makes about 450 ml (3/4 pint)

INGREDIENTS

250 ml (8 fl oz) milk
1 vanilla pod, split lengthways
3 egg yolks
75 g (2 1/2 oz) caster sugar
30 g (1 oz) plain flour, sifted

1 Scald the milk in a pan, then add the vanilla pod, cover, and leave to infuse for about 20 minutes. Meanwhile, beat the egg yolks and sugar together until thick and lemon-coloured. Whisk in the flour until just mixed.

2 Remove the vanilla pod from the milk. Transfer the egg-yolk mixture to a heavy-based saucepan and slowly pour in the milk, beating or whisking constantly, until well combined.

3 Bring to a boil over medium heat, stirring constantly, then simmer until the mixture is very thick. Transfer to a bowl and rub the surface with a piece of chilled butter or place greaseproof paper on top to prevent a skin from forming.

GARNISHES & DECORATIONS

All dishes are made instantly more appealing and appetizing when they are garnished or decorated. Even a sprig of parsley or a few chopped herbs sprinkled over a dish before it is served will give it a professional and attractive finish. Here are some simple yet stunning ideas for garnishing and decorating the savoury and sweet dishes in this book. They are all eye-catching – and easy to make.

★

TOMATO ROSES

With a very sharp, small knife or a vegetable peeler, peel a continuous strip of tomato skin in a spiral. Roll up into the shape of a rose.

PARMESAN SHAVINGS

Slowly pass a vegetable peeler over one of the edges of a block of fresh Parmesan cheese to produce thick shavings.

LIME BOWS

Slice a lime across into 5-mm (1/4-in) slices, then cut each slice into 6 segments. Use 2 segments to make a bow and finish with a sprig of dill.

VEGETABLE RIBBONS

Cut 5-mm (1/4-in) wide strips from red pepper skin, and from the green parts of leeks. Blanch in boiling water for about 1 minute to soften, then refresh in cold water. Use the strips to tie up filo pastry parcels and dolmades.

CARROT & CUCUMBER FENCES

Cut 3-mm (1/8-in) thickness of skin from a cucumber and 3-mm (1/8-in) thick slices from a carrot. Trim each to about 5 cm (2 in) long. Using a sharp knife, cut out 3 sharp points at one end. Trim the other end straight across.

SPRING ONION & CAPER FLORETS

Slice spring onions into 1-cm (¹/2-in) pieces. Top 3 fanned pieces with a caper.

ANCHOVY CURLS

Drain and dry anchovy fillets, then wrap each fillet around a caper. Tuck a tiny red pepper diamond into each curl.

CHOCOLATE-COATED FRUIT

Holding small fruit, such as strawberries, cherries, or grapes, by their stalks, dip halfway into melted chocolate. Leave to set on parchment paper.

OLIVE CUPS & RINGS

Make small angled cuts around the middle of a pimiento-stuffed green olive. Pull the halves apart. Cut stoned black olives into 5-mm (¹/4-in) slices.

PICKLED GINGER ROSES

Take 4 slices of Japanese pickled ginger. Curl 1 slice to form the centre and then wrap each of the remaining pieces around it to make the shape of a rose.

CUCUMBER TWISTS

Using a canelle knife, cut lengthways grooves in a cucumber. Cut crossways into 3-mm (¹/8-in) slices and cut halfway across each slice. Twist the cut ends away from each other. Tuck a few twists into each other to form a flower shape.

GHERKIN FANS

Make 4 lengthways cuts in small gherkins, up to 5 mm (¹/4 in) away from one end. Fan the slices out by gently separating the slices.

ORANGE PEEL CURLS

Using a canelle knife, cut strips of peel to the desired length. Curl round the handle of a wooden spoon.

CARROT FLOWERS

Using a canelle knife, cut several lengthways grooves in a carrot. Cut the carrot crossways into 5-mm (¹/4-in) slices to form flower shapes.

Author's Notes

★

Measurements

Metric and Imperial measurements have been calculated separately. Use only one set of measures, because they are not exact equivalents. All spoon measurements are level.

Milk

I always use low-fat milk. It doesn't affect the taste and is much healthier.

Sugar

Unless otherwise specified, granulated sugar is used in the recipes.

Olive oil

I always use extra-virgin olive oil, made from the first cold pressing – this should be indicated on the label of the bottle.

Eggs

Whenever eggs are included in recipes, they are always used at room temperature.

Juice

When lemon, lime, or orange juice is called for in a recipe, I prefer to use freshly squeezed juice, which gives a much better flavour.

Drained yogurt

I like to use drained yogurt in some dips and sauces because it adds a smooth rich texture, and is easy to make at home. The flavour, texture, and fat content are concentrated – even low-fat yogurt will seem creamy when prepared by this method.

To make drained yogurt, place a large sieve over a bowl and line the sieve with a double thickness of muslin. Spoon 500 ml (16 fl oz) plain low-fat yogurt into the sieve, cover, and refrigerate overnight or for several hours. The yogurt will lose up to half its volume in water into the bowl and become thick and creamy.

Fromage blanc

This is a fresh, very soft cream cheese with the consistency of soured cream. It can be used in cooking or served with fruit.

To make fromage blanc, blend together 250 g (8 oz) low-fat cottage cheese with 3 tbsp plain low-fat yogurt until smooth.

Dried mushrooms

The concentrated flavour of dried mushrooms adds an intense savouriness to cooked dishes, and just a small amount can transform a dish.

To rehydrate dried mushrooms, place the mushrooms in a bowl and pour boiling water over them to cover. Let stand for 15–30 minutes until softened. Place a sieve over a bowl and line the sieve with muslin or paper towels. Tip the mushrooms into the sieve and let the liquid drain through; reserve the liquid for use in the recipe. Rinse the mushrooms in several changes of water, squeeze dry, and prepare according to the recipe.

Extracts

I prefer to use extracts because they are derived from the natural product, rather than flavourings, which are made from chemically-derived products.

Almond extract is made from bitter almond oil mixed with ethyl alcohol. It has an intense flavour, and only a very small amount is needed to give a strong almond taste.

Vanilla extract is a clear brown liquid with a sweet, fragrant aroma. It is made by mixing chopped vanilla beans in an alcohol and water solution in order to extract the flavour. Vanilla extract has a concentrated flavour, and so, only a few drops are needed. Check the label before buying: if it is labelled "vanilla flavouring", or "vanilla flavoured", it has been made from synthetic vanillin, which can leave a bitter aftertaste.

Remember that extracts can also sometimes be called essences.

Seasoned rice vinegar

This is the vinegar which is traditionally used to add piquancy to the rice when making sushi.

To make seasoned rice vinegar, dissolve 1 tbsp sugar and 2 tsp salt in 4 tbsp rice vinegar. Heat over medium heat to dissolve the sugar and salt, and let cool before using.

Baking stone

The best pizzas are made in brick ovens. A baking stone, when preheated in an oven set to 230°C (450°F, Gas 8), conducts heat in the same way as a brick oven floor. It is a heavy flat, round or rectangular stone, available from kitchen shops, and the pizza is placed directly on it in the oven.

Index

Acknowledgments

★

Photographers' assistants Nick Allen and Sid Sideris
Home economist Maddalena Bastianelli
Typesetting Axis Design
Production Consultant Lorraine Baird
Text Film by Disc to Print (UK) Limited

Author's photograph David Goldes (USA)

Author's appreciation

A few of my colleagues were incredibly helpful to me as I put together this
collection. Above all, I would like to thank Anne Trager, who tested many of the
recipes, and for her duck and lamb terrines (pages 110–112), and marvellous fillings
for gougères (pages 50–51). Elaine Corn gave me her recipe for
Brandied Liver Pâté (page 110), and gave me much good advice about cakes.
My directions for making Gravadlax (page 104) are based on those given to
me by my friend and colleague, Susan Herrmann Loomis, while the Mincemeat
Tartlets on page 118 were inspired by Deborah Madison. Much of my inspiration
for Middle-Eastern dishes, such as the meatballs (page 99), I owe to Claudia Roden.

Thanks also to Octavia Wiseman at Abner Stein Literary Agency,
and to Amy Carroll, Eric Treuillé, Jeni Wright, Shirin Patel, and
the rest of the team at Carroll & Brown.
And, as always, to my husband, Bill Grantham.